UKULELE

THE BEST SONGS EVER

ISBN 978-1-5400-3419-9

HAL•LEONARD®

Visit Hal Leonard Online at
www.halleonard.com

Contact us:
Hal Leonard
7777 West Bluemound Road
Milwaukee, WI 53213
Email: info@halleonard.com

In Europe, contact:
Hal Leonard Europe Limited
42 Wigmore Street
Marylebone, London, W1U 2RN
Email: info@halleonardeurope.com

In Australia, contact:
Hal Leonard Australia Pty. Ltd.
4 Lentara Court
Cheltenham, Victoria, 3192 Australia
Email: info@halleonard.com.au

All I Ask of You

from THE PHANTOM OF THE OPERA
Music by Andrew Lloyd Webber
Lyrics by Charles Hart
Additional Lyrics by Richard Stilgoe

Chorus

Raoul:

say you'll share with me one love, one life - time; let me lead you from your

sol - i - tude. __ Say you need me with you, here be - side you,

an - y - where __ you go, let me go too. Chris - tine, __ that's all I ask of

Chorus

Christine:

Say you'll share with me one love, one life - time; say the word and I will
you.

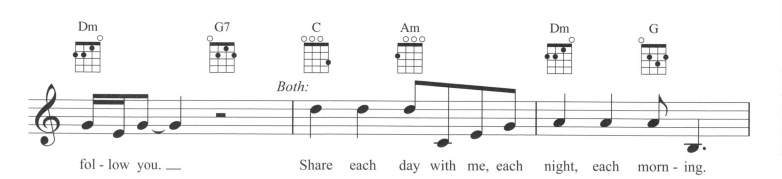

Both:

fol - low you. __ Share each day with me, each night, each morn - ing.

Christine:

Raoul:

Say you love me!

You know I do.

Interlude

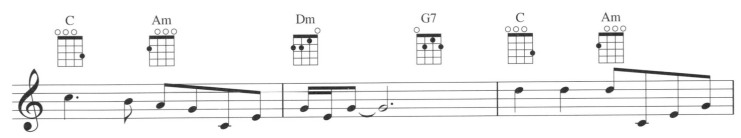

Both: *molto rit.* *a tempo*

Love me, that's all I ask of you.
(Instrumental)

Outro

largo

An - y - where _ you go, let me go too;

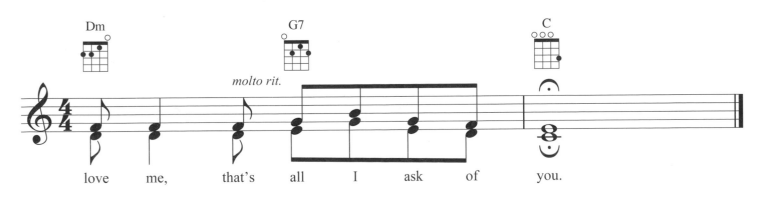

molto rit.

love me, that's all I ask of you.

All the Things You Are

from VERY WARM FOR MAY
Lyrics by Oscar Hammerstein II
Music by Jerome Kern

Always

Words and Music by Irving Berlin

Bewitched

from PAL JOEY
Words by Lorenz Hart
Music by Richard Rodgers

First note

Verse
Moderately

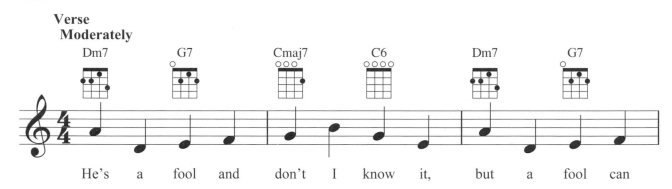

He's a fool and don't I know it, but a fool can

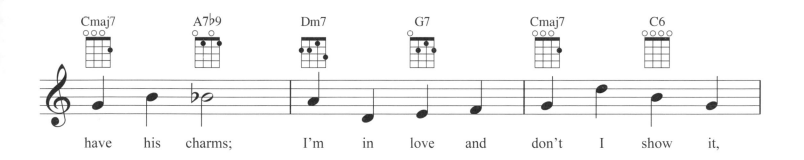

have his charms; I'm in love and don't I show it,

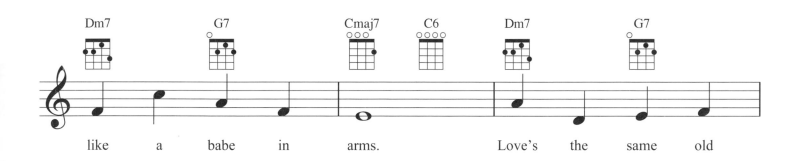

like a babe in arms. Love's the same old

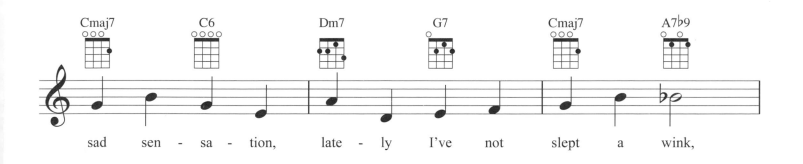

sad sen-sa-tion, late-ly I've not slept a wink,

since this half - pint im - i - ta - tion put me on the

Chorus
Slowly

blink. I'm wild a - gain, be - guiled a - gain, a

sim - per - ing, whim - per - ing child a - gain; be - witched, both - ered and be -

wil - dered am I. _____

Could-n't sleep and would-n't sleep, when love came and told me I

should-n't sleep; be - witched, both - ered and be - wil - dered am

At Last

Lyric by Mack Gordon
Music by Harry Warren

First note

Verse

Slowly, in 2

1. At last _____ my love ___ has come a -
(2.) last _____ the skies ___ a - bove are

long, _____ my lone - ly days are o - ver ___
blue, _____ my heart ___ was wrapped in clo - ver ___

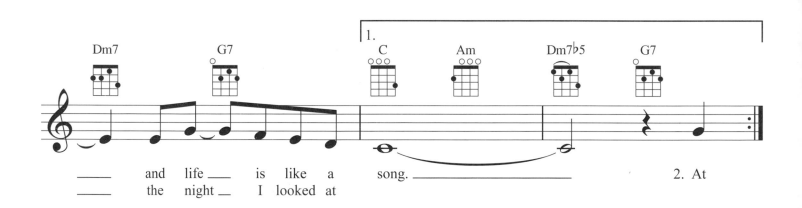

____ and life ___ is like a song. _____ 2. At
____ the night ___ I looked at

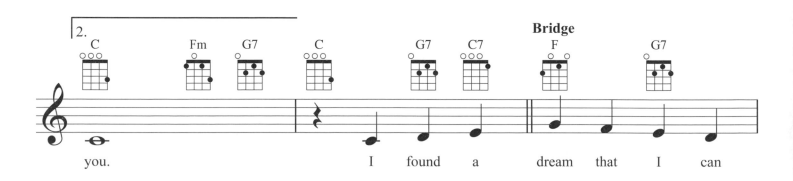

you. I found a dream that I can

speak to, _____ a dream that I can call my own. _____ I found a

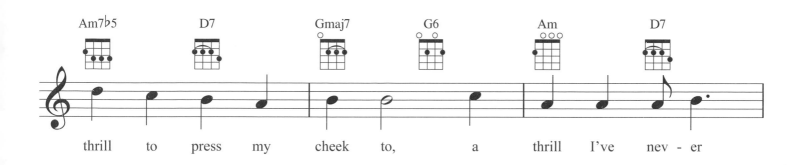

thrill to press my cheek to, a thrill I've nev - er

Outro-Verse

known. You smiled _____ and then ___ the spell was

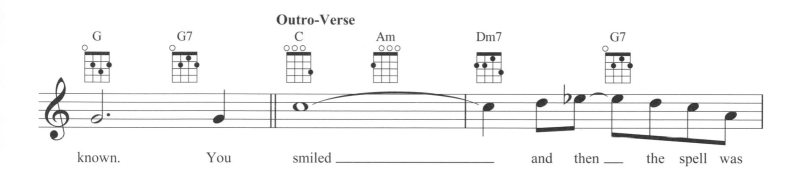

cast, _____ and here ___ we are in heav - en, _____

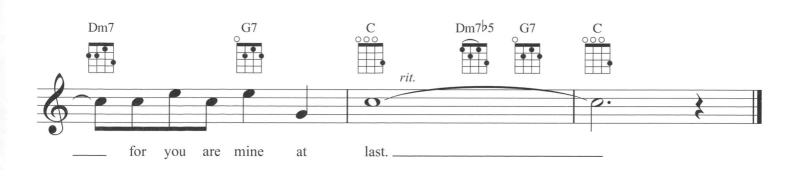

_____ for you are mine at last. _____

Billie Jean

Words and Music by Michael Jackson

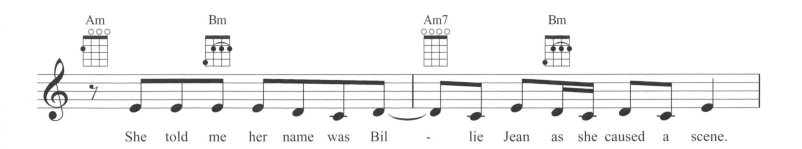

She told me her name was Bil – lie Jean as she caused a scene.

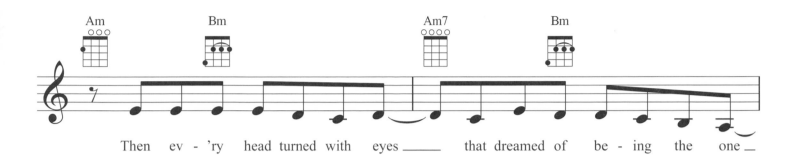

Then ev – 'ry head turned with eyes _____ that dreamed of be – ing the one _____

_____ who will dance on the floor in the round.

Pre-Chorus

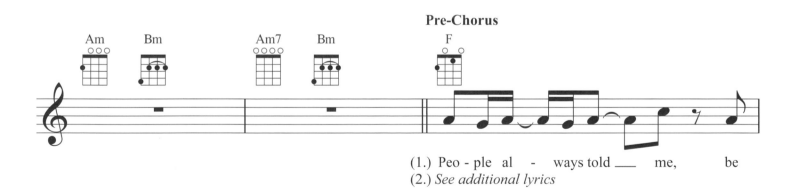

(1.) Peo – ple al – ways told _____ me, be
(2.) *See additional lyrics*

care – ful of what you do. Don't go a – round _____ break – in' young girls' hearts. _____

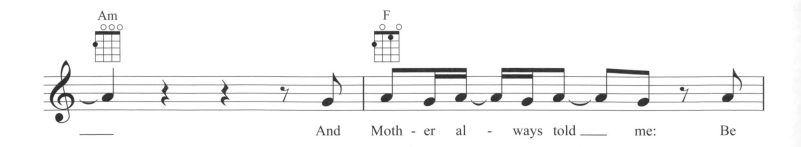

And Moth - er al - ways told ___ me: Be

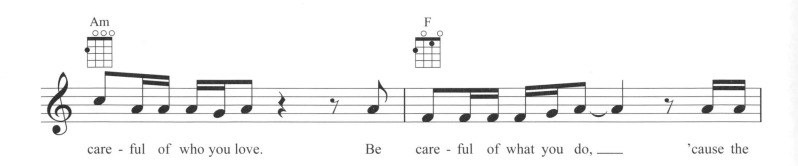

care - ful of who you love. Be care - ful of what you do, ___ 'cause the

Chorus

lie be - comes _ the truth. Hey. _____ Bil - lie Jean ___ is

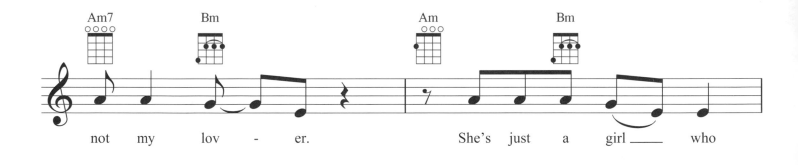

not my lov - er. She's just a girl ___ who

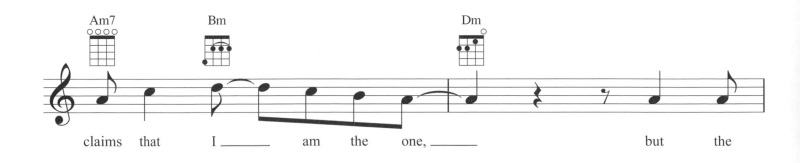

claims that I _____ am the one, _____ but the

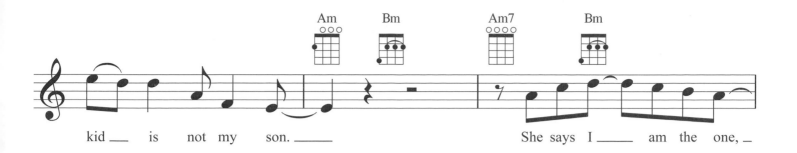

kid __ is not my son. _____ She says I _____ am the one, _

_____ but the kid __ is not my son. _____

1.

2.

Outro

Repeat and fade

Bil - lie Jean _ is not my lov - er.

Additional Lyrics

2. For forty days and for forty nights, law was on her side.
   But who can stand when she's in demand, her schemes and plans,
   'Cause we danced on the floor in the round?
   So take my strong advice: Just remember to always think twice.
   She told my baby we'd danced till three,
   And she looked at me, then showed a photo.
   My baby cried; his eyes were like mine,
   'Cause we danced on the floor in the round.

Pre-Chorus: People always told me: Be careful of what you do.
   Don't go around breakin' young girls' hearts.
   But you came and stood right by me, just a smell of sweet perfume.
   This happened much too soon; she called me to her room. Hey.

Blue Skies

from BETSY
Words and Music by Irving Berlin

1. Blue skies _____ smil-ing at me, _____
2. Blue - birds _____ sing-ing a song, _____
3. Blue days _____ all of them gone, _____

_____ noth-ing but blue skies _____ do I see. _____
_____ noth-ing but blue - birds _____ from now on. _____
_____ noth-ing but blue skies _____ from now on. _____

Bridge

Fine

Nev-er saw the sun shin-ing so bright,

nev-er saw things go-ing so right. No-tic-ing the days

D.C. al Fine

hur-ry-ing by, when you're in love, my how they fly.

Bohemian Rhapsody

Words and Music by Freddie Mercury

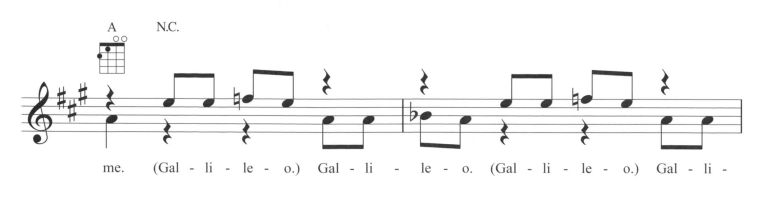

me. (Gal - li - le - o.) Gal - li - le - o. (Gal - li - le - o.) Gal - li -

le - o, Gal - li - le - o, Fig - a - ro, mag - ni - fi - co. _____

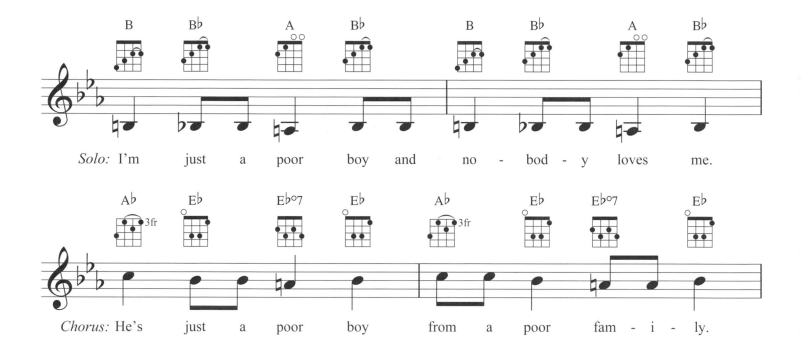

Solo: I'm just a poor boy and no - bod - y loves me.

Chorus: He's just a poor boy from a poor fam - i - ly.

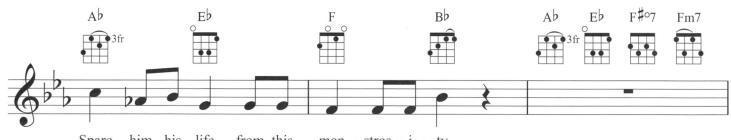

Spare him his life from this mon - stros - i - ty.

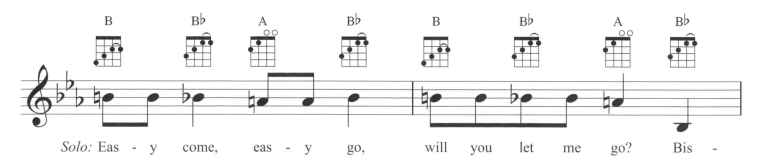

Solo: Eas - y come, eas - y go, will you let me go? Bis -

Chorus:

mil - lah! No, we will not let you go. (Let him go!) _____ Bis - mil - lah! We

will not let you go. (Let him go!) _____ Bis - mil - lah! We

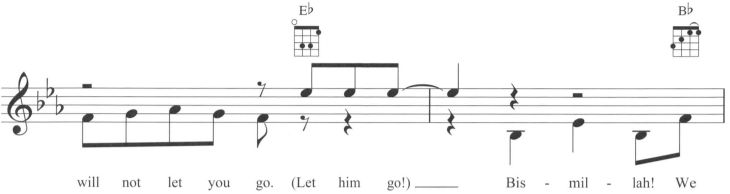

(Let me go!) _____ (Let me go!) _
will not let you go. Will not let you go.

_____ (Let me go!) _____ Ah. _____
Will not let you go.

Solo: *Chorus:*
No, no, no, no, no, no, no. (Oh, ma - ma mi - a, ma - ma mi - a.) Ma - ma

25

mi - a, let me go. Be - el - ze - bub has a dev - il put a - side for

me, for me, _____ for me. _____

So you think you can stone me and spit in my eye. _____

So you think you can love me and leave me to

die. _____ Oh, _____ ba - by, _____ can't do this to me,

ba - by. _____ Just got - ta get out, just got - ta get right out - ta

Body and Soul

Words by Edward Heyman, Robert Sour and Frank Eyton
Music by John Green

you'd turn a - way ro - mance.

Are you pre - tend - ing? It looks like the end - ing un -

less I could have one more chance to prove, dear.

Outro-Verse

My life a wreck you're mak - ing, you know I'm yours for

just the tak - ing; I'd glad - ly sur - ren - der

my - self to you, bod - y and soul!

Can't Help Falling in Love

Words and Music by George David Weiss, Hugo Peretti and Luigi Creatore

Defying Gravity

from the Broadway Musical WICKED
Music and Lyrics by Stephen Schwartz

Crazy

Words and Music by Willie Nelson

First note

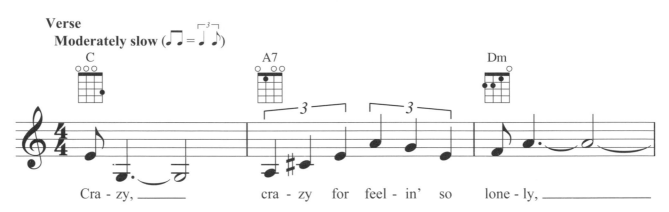

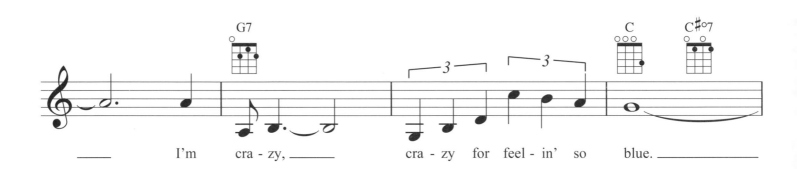

Edelweiss

from THE SOUND OF MUSIC
Lyrics by Oscar Hammerstein II
Music by Richard Rodgers

Bridge

Blos - som of snow, may you bloom and

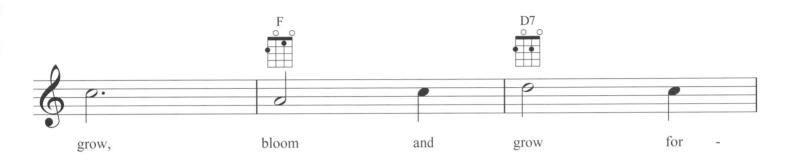

grow, bloom and grow for -

Chorus

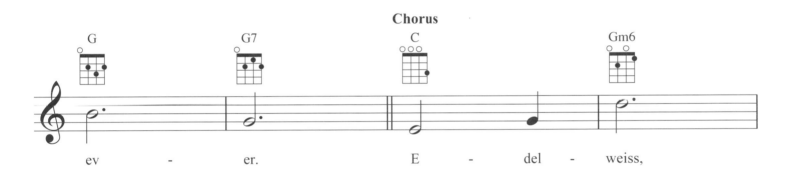

ev - er. E - del - weiss,

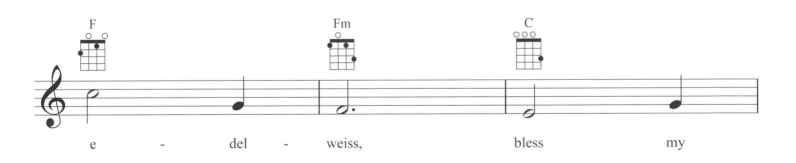

e - del - weiss, bless my

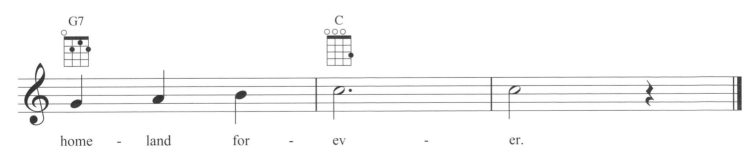

home - land for - ev - er.

Every Breath You Take

Music and Lyrics by Sting

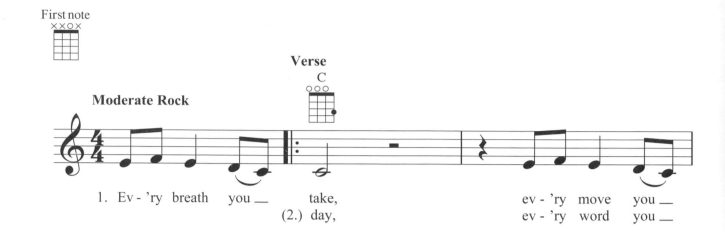

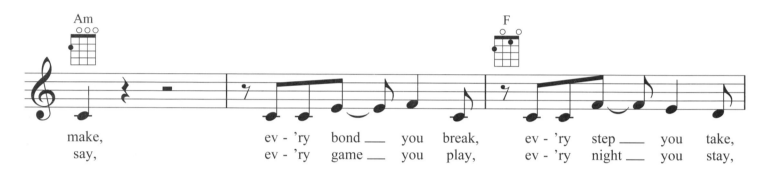

me.　　　　　　　　　　　　　　How my poor heart _____ aches _____

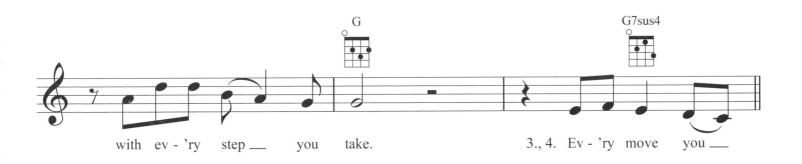

with ev - 'ry step ___ you take.　　　　　　　3., 4. Ev - 'ry move you ___

Verse

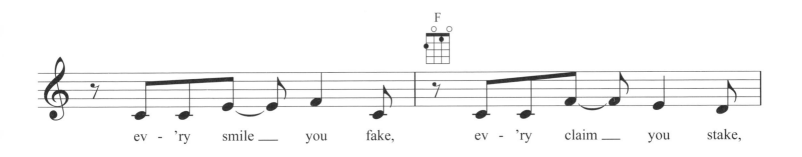

make,　　　　　　　ev - 'ry vow you ___ break,

ev - 'ry smile ___ you fake,　　ev - 'ry claim ___ you stake,

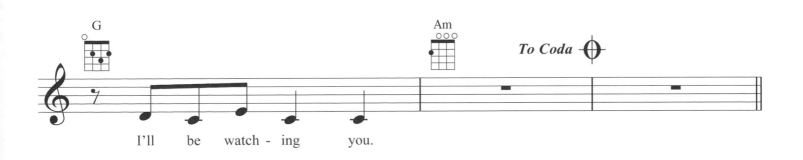

To Coda ⊕

I'll be watch - ing you.

Bridge

Since you've gone, ___ I've been lost ___ with - out _____ a trace.

I dream at night, I can on - ly see _____ your face.

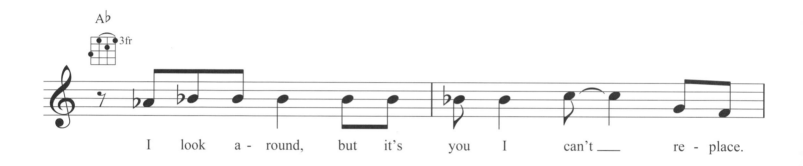

I look a - round, but it's you I can't ____ re - place.

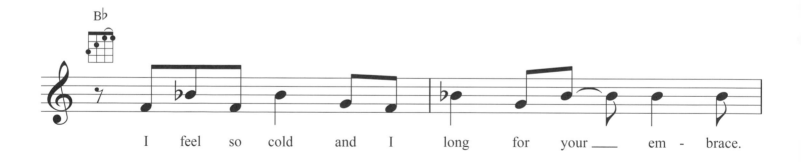

I feel so cold and I long for your ___ em - brace.

I keep cry - ing, ba - by, ba - by, please. ___

Interlude

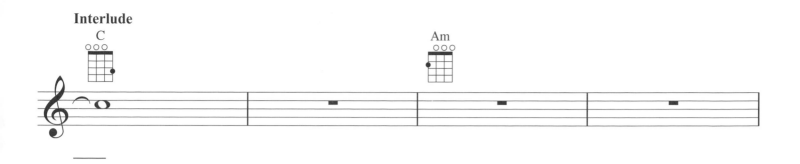

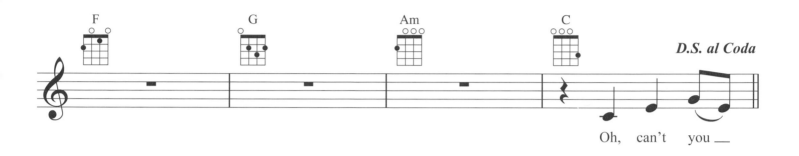

D.S. al Coda

Oh, can't you ___

Coda   **Outro**

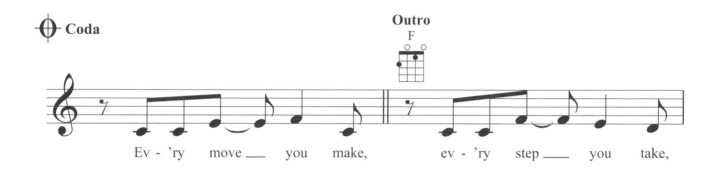

Ev - 'ry move ___ you make,   ev - 'ry step ___ you take,

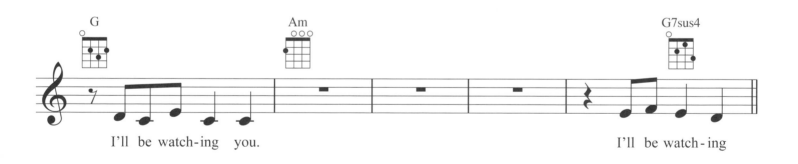

I'll be watch-ing you.   I'll be watch-ing

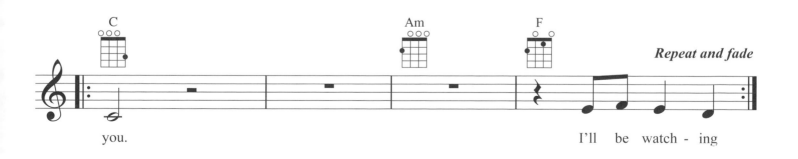

Repeat and fade

you.   I'll be watch - ing

Fly Me to the Moon
(In Other Words)

Words and Music by Bart Howard

First note

Verse
Medium Swing

Am   Dm

1., 3. Fly   me   to   the   moon ___ and   let   me
2., 4. Fill   my   heart with song ___ and   let   me

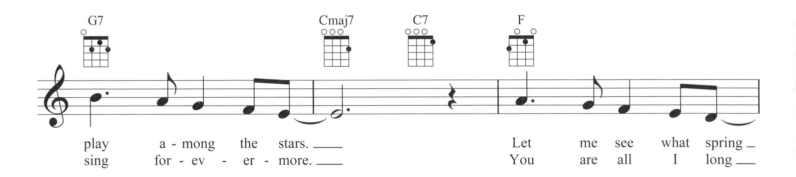

G7   Cmaj7   C7   F

play   a - mong the   stars. ___   Let   me   see   what   spring ___
sing   for - ev - er - more. ___   You   are   all   I   long ___

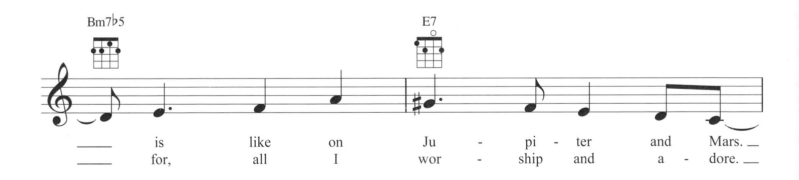

Bm7♭5   E7

___   is   like   on   Ju - pi - ter   and   Mars. ___
___   for,   all   I   wor - ship   and   a - dore. ___

Am   A7   Dm   G7   *To Coda* ⊕

___   In   oth - er   words, ___   hold   my
___   In   oth - er   words, ___   please   be

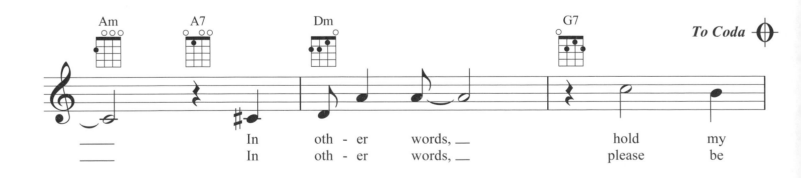

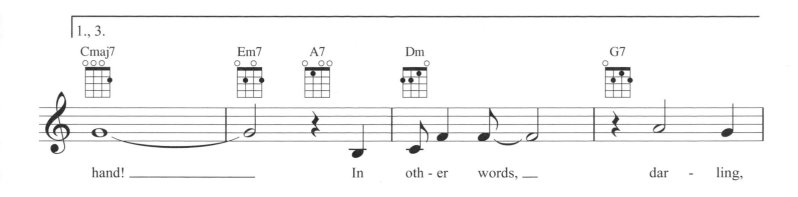

hand! _____ In oth-er words, __ dar - ling,

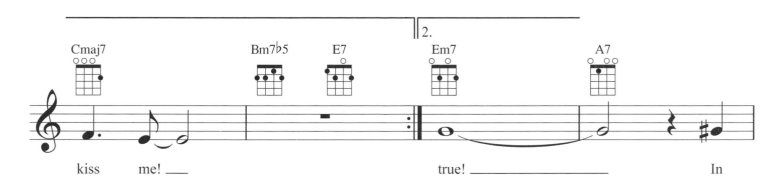

kiss me! ___ true! _____ In

D.C. al Coda
(with repeat)

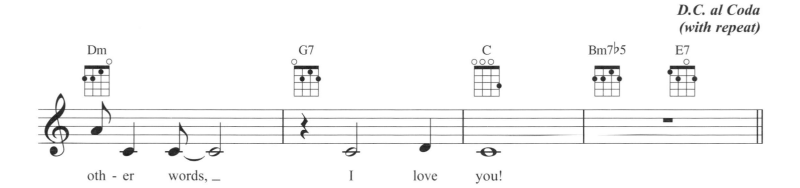

oth - er words, __ I love you!

Coda

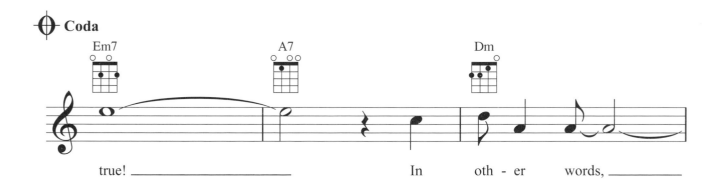

true! _____ In oth - er words, _____

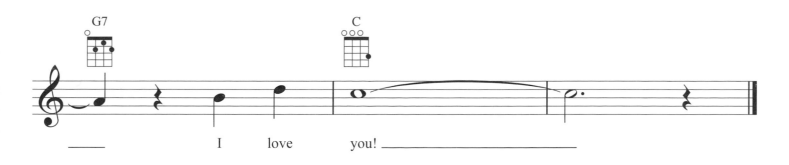

_____ I love you! _____

Georgia on My Mind

Words by Stuart Gorrell
Music by Hoagy Carmichael

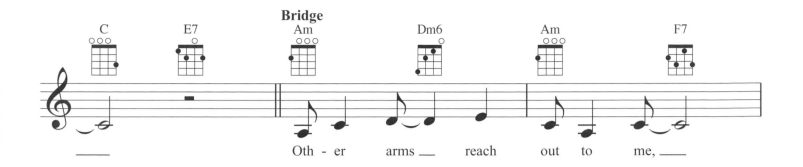

Bridge

Oth - er arms ___ reach out to me, ___

oth - er eyes ___ smile ten - der - ly. ___ Still, in peace - ful

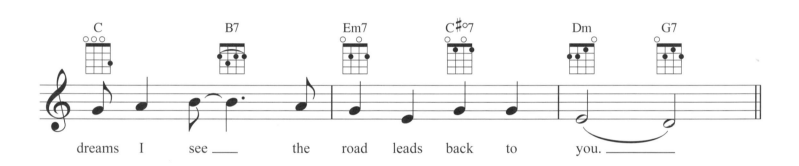

dreams I see ___ the road leads back to you. ___

Outro-Chorus

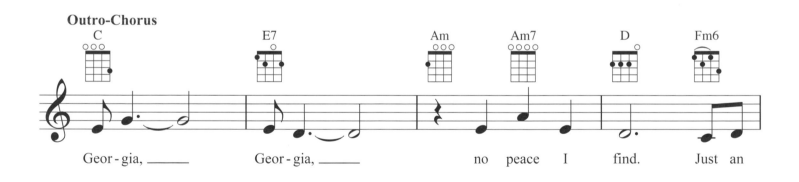

Geor - gia, ___ Geor - gia, ___ no peace I find. Just an

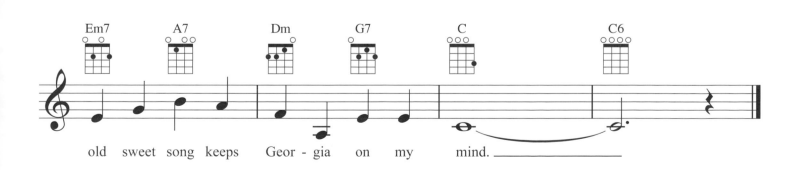

old sweet song keeps Geor - gia on my mind. ___

Hallelujah

Words and Music by Leonard Cohen

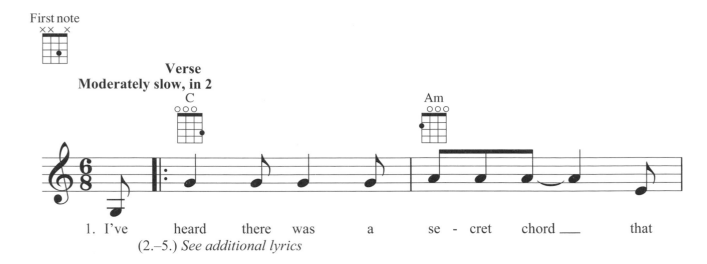

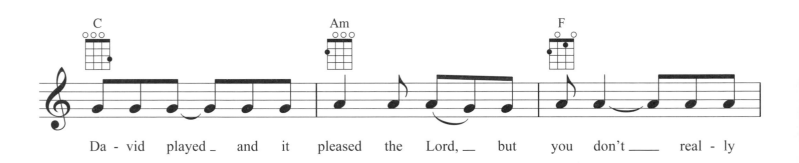

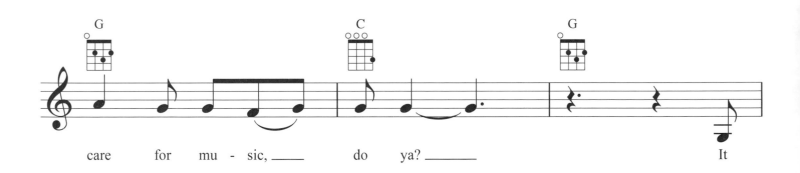

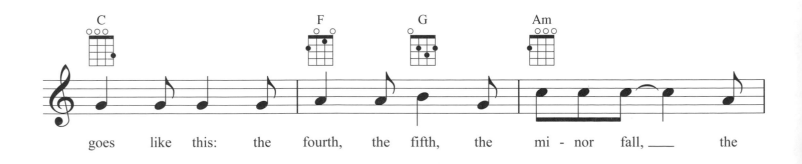

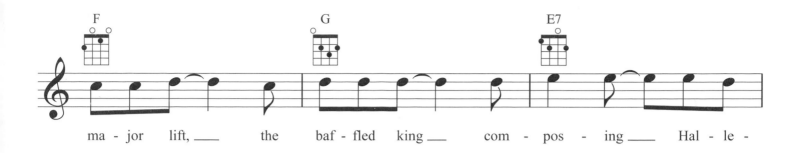

ma - jor lift, ____ the baf - fled king ____ com - pos - ing ____ Hal - le -

Chorus

lu - jah. ____ Hal - le - lu - jah, _____ hal - le -

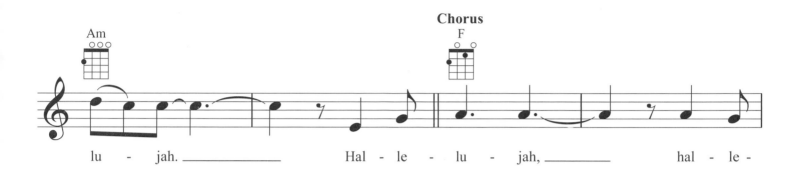

lu - jah, _____ hal - le - lu - jah, _____ hal - le -

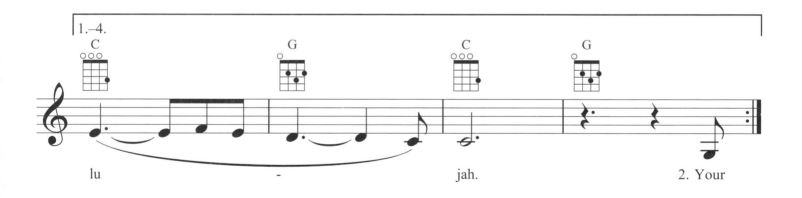

lu - jah. 2. Your

Outro-Chorus

lu - jah. Hal - le - lu - jah. ____ Hal - le -

lu - jah. _____ Hal - le - lu - jah. _____ Hal - le -

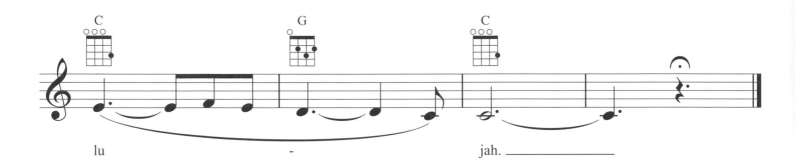

lu - jah. _____

Additional Lyrics

2. Your faith was strong but you needed proof.
   You saw her bathing on the roof.
   Her beauty and the moonlight overthrew ya.
   She tied you to a kitchen chair.
   She broke your throne, she cut your hair.
   And from your lips she drew the Hallelujah.

3. Maybe I have been here before.
   I know this room, I've walked this floor.
   I used to live alone before I knew ya.
   I've seen your flag on the marble arch.
   Love is not a vict'ry march.
   It's a cold and it's a broken Hallelujah.

4. There was a time you let me know
   What's real and going on below.
   But now you never show it to me, do ya?
   And remember when I moved in you.
   The holy dark was movin', too,
   And every breath we drew was Hallelujah.

5. Maybe there's a God above,
   And all I ever learned from love
   Was how to shoot at someone who outdrew ya.
   And it's not a cry you can hear at night.
   It's not somebody who's seen the light.
   It's a cold and it's a broken Hallelujah.

The Girl from Ipanema

(Garôta de Ipanema)

Music by Antonio Carlos Jobim
English Words by Norman Gimbel
Original Words by Vinicius de Moraes

First note

Verse
Moderate Bossa Nova

1. Tall and tan and young ___ and love - ly, the girl ___
2. When she walks she's like ___ a sam - ba that

___ from I - pa - ne - ma goes walk - ing, and when ___
swings so cool and sways ___ so gen - tle, that when ___

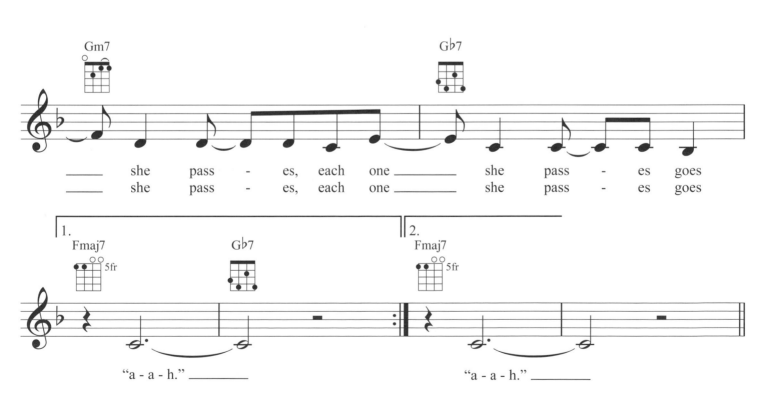

___ she pass - es, each one ___ she pass - es goes
___ she pass - es, each one ___ she pass - es goes

1.
"a - a - h." ___

2.
"a - a - h." ___

Bridge

Oh, _____ but I watch her so sad - ly. _____

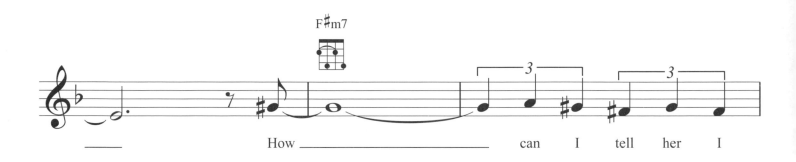

_____ How _____ can I tell her I

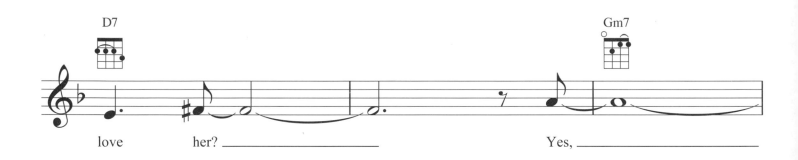

love her? _____ Yes, _____

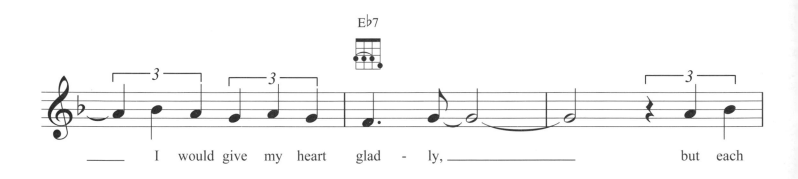

_____ I would give my heart glad - ly, _____ but each

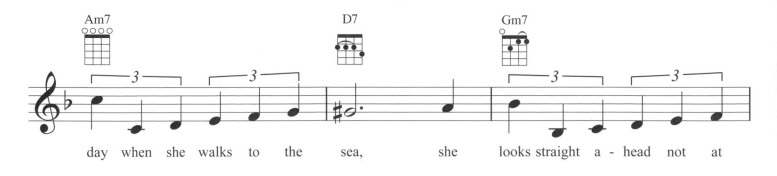

day when she walks to the sea, she looks straight a - head not at

Outro-Verse

me. Tall and tan and young _____ and love - ly, the girl _____

_____ from I - pa - ne - ma goes walk - ing, and when _____

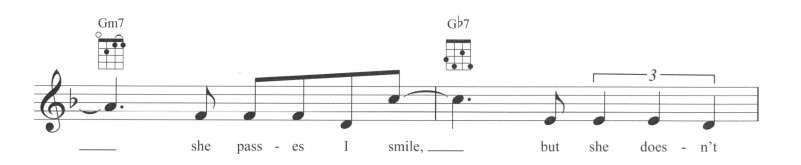

_____ she pass - es I smile, _____ but she does - n't

see. She just does - n't see.

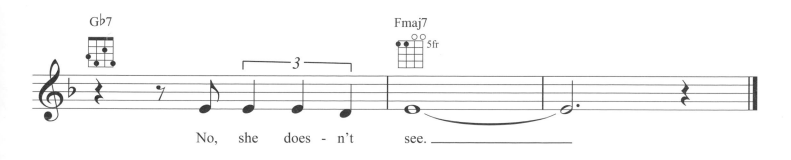

No, she does - n't see. _____

Happy

from DESPICABLE ME 2
Words and Music by Pharrell Williams

_____ you feel _____ like that's what you wan - na do. _____

 Bridge

Bring me down, _____ can't noth - in' bring me down;

_____ your love is too high. Bring me down, _____ can't noth - in'

1.

bring me down. _____ (Let me tell you now.)

Chorus

2., 3.

_____ I said... (Be - cause I'm hap - py.) Clap a - long if _____

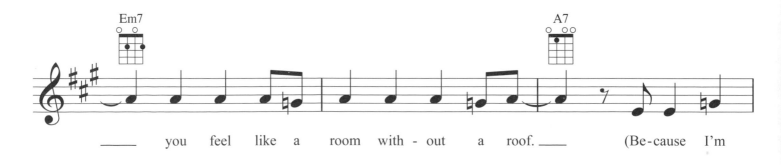

_____ you feel like a room with - out a roof. _____ (Be-cause I'm

Here's That Rainy Day

Words by Johnny Burke
Music by Jimmy Van Heusen

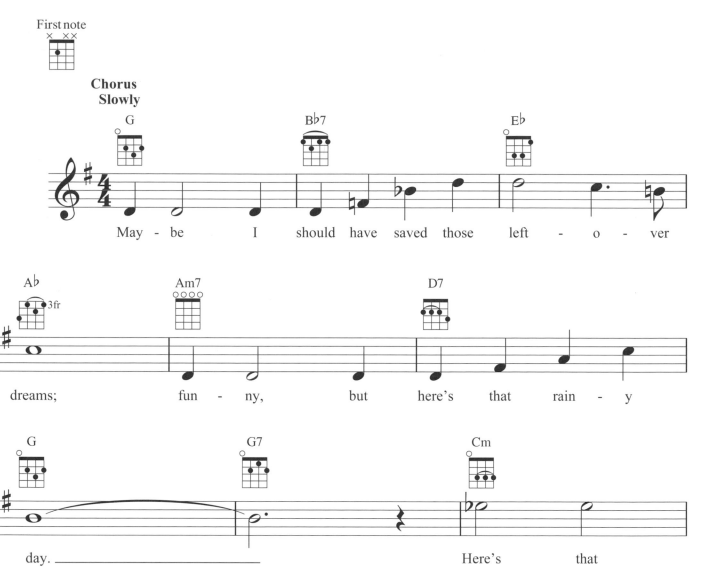

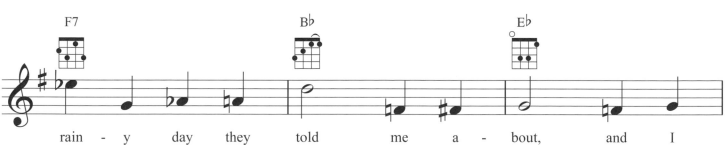

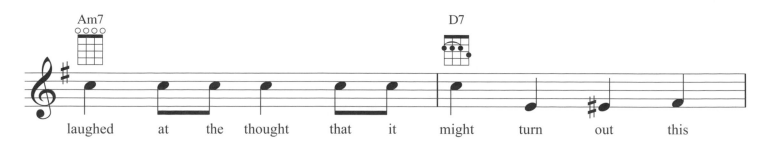

way. _____

Where is that worn - out wish that I threw a - side, af - ter it brought my lov - er near? _____ Fun - ny how love be - comes a cold rain - y day. Fun - ny that rain - y day is here. _____

Hey Jude

Words and Music by John Lennon and Paul McCartney

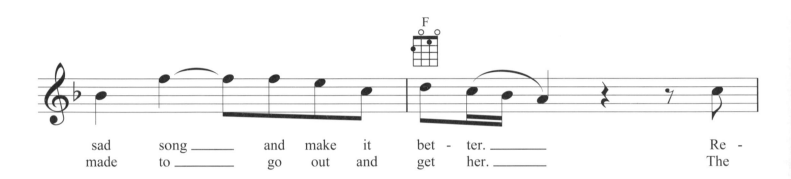

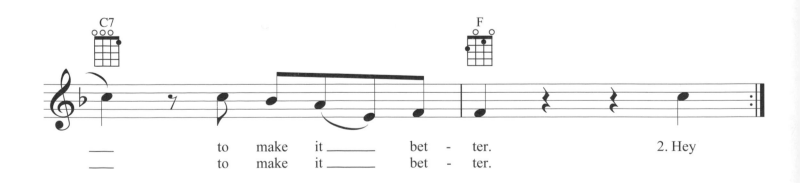

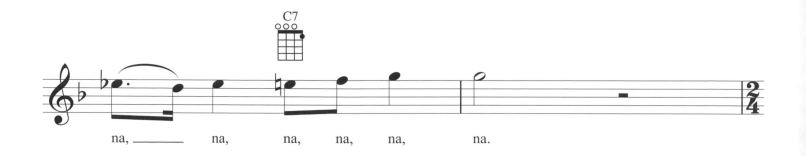

na, _____ na, na, na, na, na.

Verse

To Coda

3., 4. Hey _ Jude, don't let me down. You have

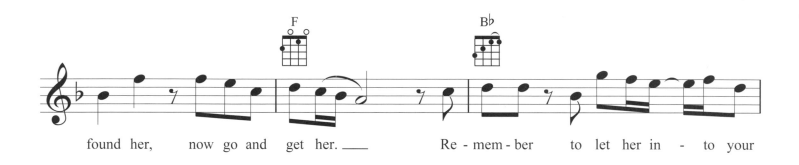

found her, now go and get her. ___ Re - mem - ber to let her in - to your

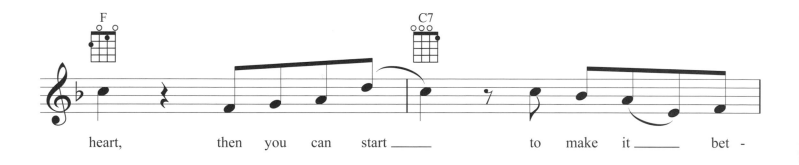

heart, then you can start _____ to make it _____ bet -

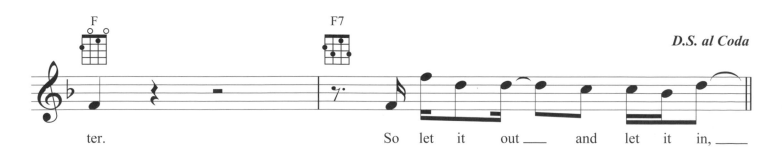

D.S. al Coda

ter. So let it out ___ and let it in, ___

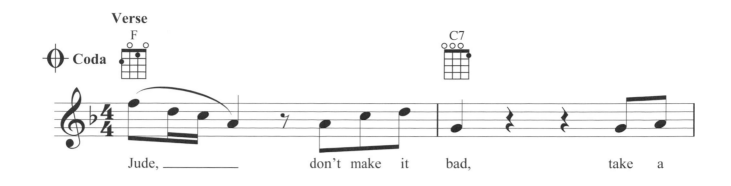

Verse

Jude, _____ don't make it bad, take a

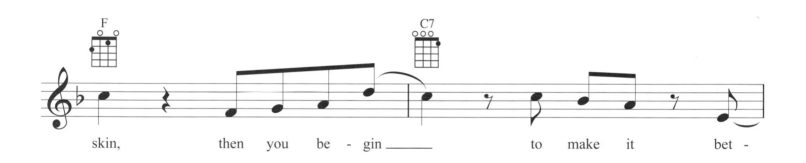

sad song and make it bet - ter. ____ Re - mem - ber to let her un - der your

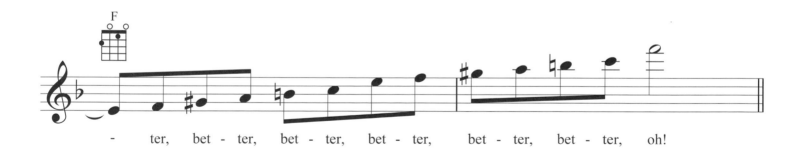

skin, then you be - gin _____ to make it bet -

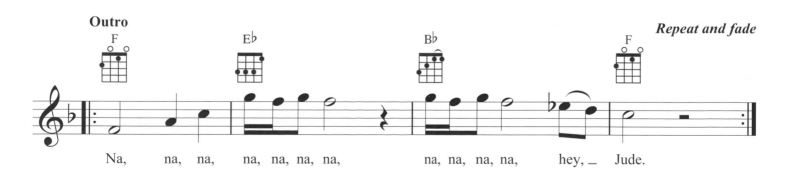

- ter, bet - ter, bet - ter, bet - ter, bet - ter, bet - ter, oh!

Outro   *Repeat and fade*

Na, na, na, na, na, na, na, na, na, na, na, hey, _ Jude.

How Deep Is the Ocean

(How High Is the Sky)

Words and Music by Irving Berlin

How far would I trav - el to be where you are? How far is the jour - ney from here to a star? And if I ev - er lost you, how much would I cry? How deep is the o - cean, how high is the sky?

I Left My Heart in San Francisco

Words by Douglass Cross
Music by George Cory

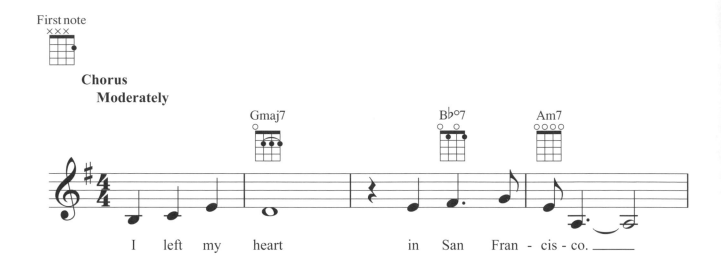

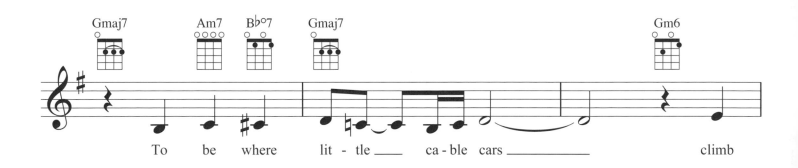

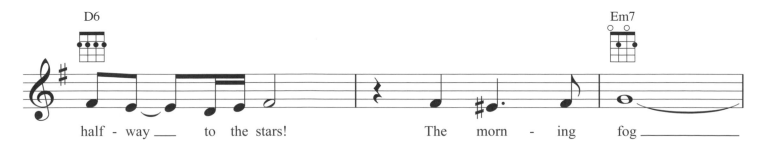

may chill the air; I don't care! My love waits

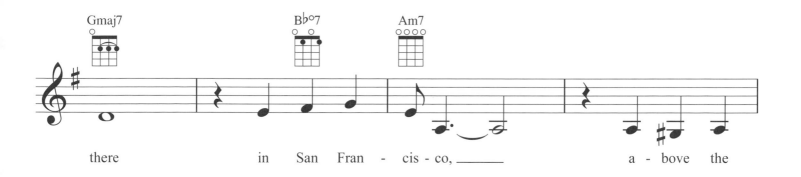

there in San Fran - cis - co, _____ a - bove the

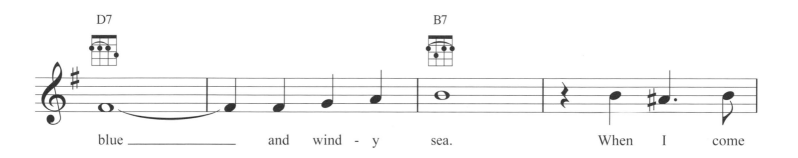

blue _____ and wind - y sea. When I come

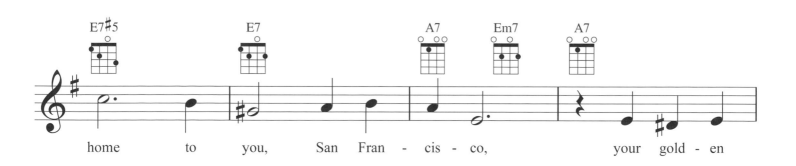

home to you, San Fran - cis - co, your gold - en

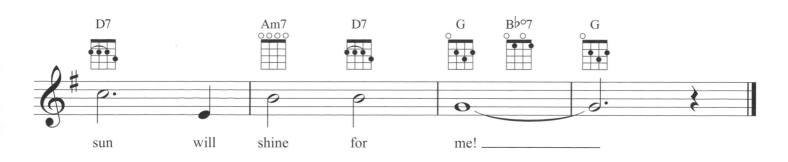

sun will shine for me! _____

I Will Always Love You

Words and Music by Dolly Parton

First note

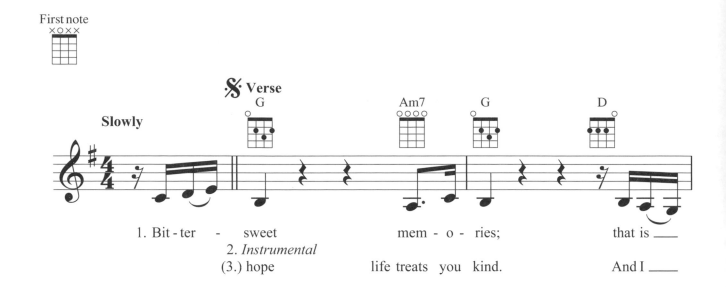

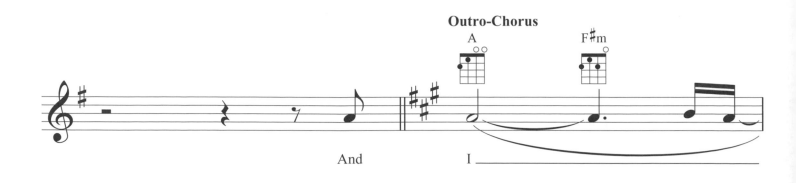

Outro-Chorus

And I _____

_____ will _ al - ways _ love _ you. _____ I _____ will al -

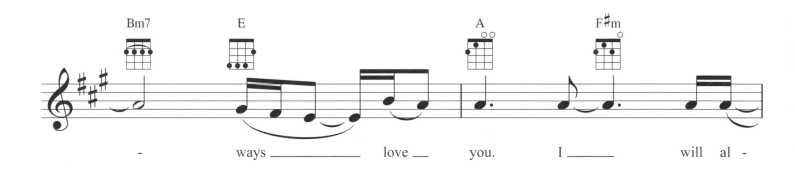

- ways _____ love _ you. I _____ will al -

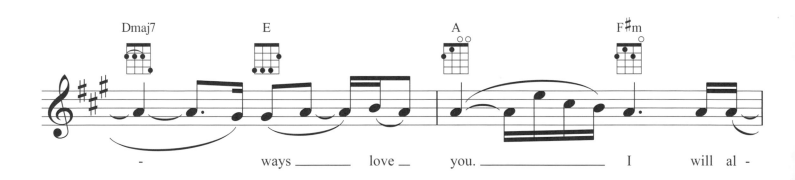

- ways _____ love _ you. _____ I will al -

- ways _____ love you.

I Dreamed a Dream

from LES MISÉRABLES

Music by Claude-Michel Schönberg
Lyrics by Alain Boublil, Jean-Marc Natel and Herbert Kretzmer

tast - ed.   But the ti - gers come at night

with their voic - es soft as thun - der,   as they tear your hope a -

part,   as they turn your dream to shame.

{ He / She } slept a sum - mer by my

side.   { He / She } filled my days with end - less won - der.

{ He / She } took my child - hood in { his / her } stride, but { he / she } was gone when au - tumn

I'll Be Seeing You

Written by Irving Kahal and Sammy Fain

Isn't It Romantic?

from the Paramount Picture LOVE ME TONIGHT
Words by Lorenz Hart
Music by Richard Rodgers

First note

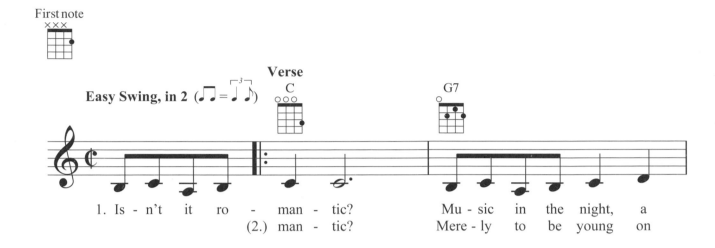

Verse

Easy Swing, in 2

1. Is - n't it ro - man - tic? Mu - sic in the night, a
(2.) man - tic? Mere - ly to be young on

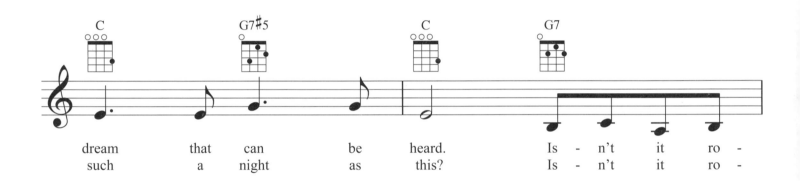

dream that can be heard. Is - n't it ro -
such a night as this? Is - n't it ro -

man - tic? Mov - ing shad - ows write the old - est mag - ic
man - tic? Ev - 'ry note that's sung is like a lov - er's

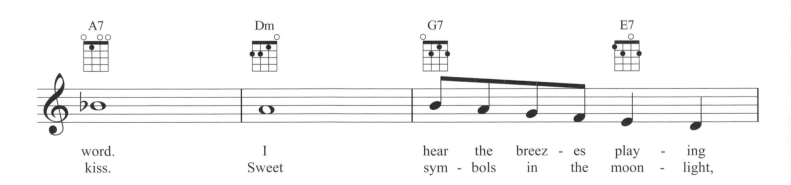

word. I hear the breez - es play - ing
kiss. Sweet sym - bols in the moon - light,

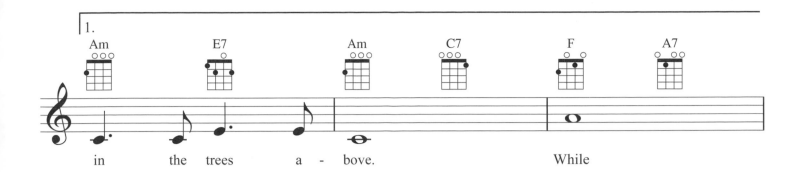

in   the   trees   a - bove.   While

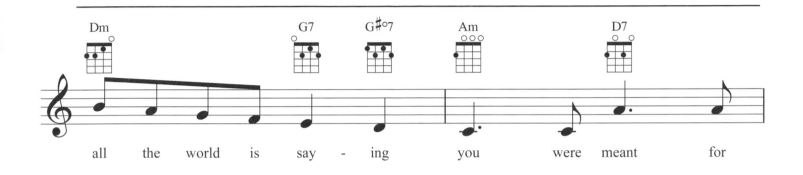

all   the   world   is   say - ing   you   were   meant   for

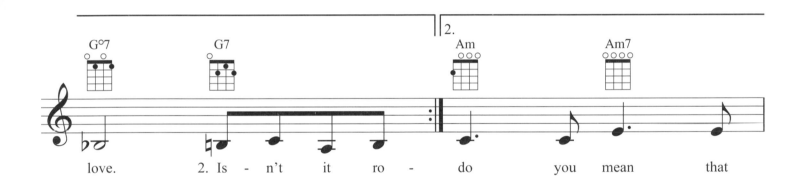

love.   2. Is - n't   it   ro - do   you   mean   that

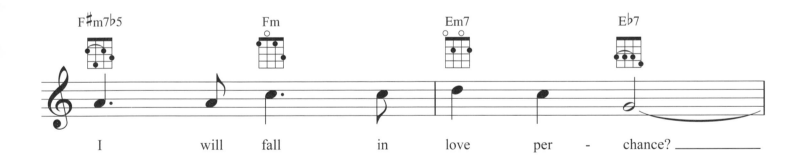

I   will   fall   in   love   per - chance? _____

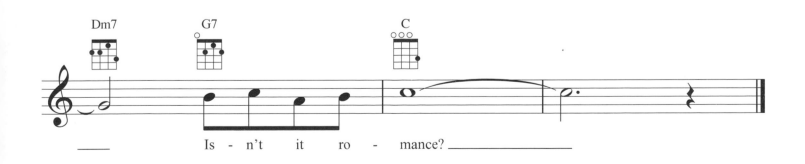

___   Is - n't   it   ro - mance? _____

It Might as Well Be Spring

from STATE FAIR
Lyrics by Oscar Hammerstein II
Music by Richard Rodgers

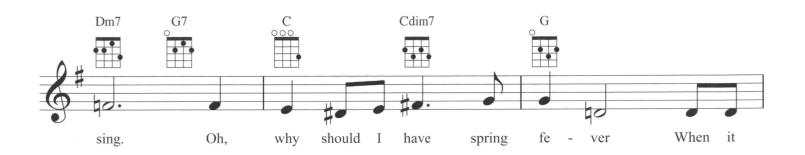

sing. Oh, why should I have spring fe - ver When it

Bridge

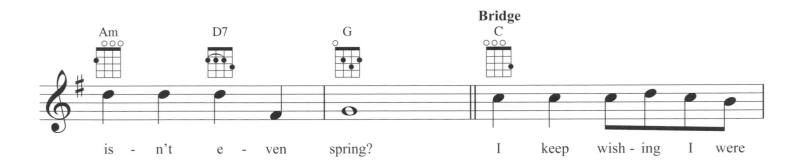

is - n't e - ven spring? I keep wish - ing I were

some - where else, walk - ing down a strange, new street,

Hear - ing words that I have nev - er heard from a { man / girl } I've yet to

Outro-Verse

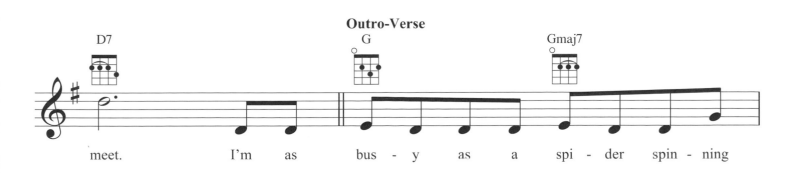

meet. I'm as bus - y as a spi - der spin - ning

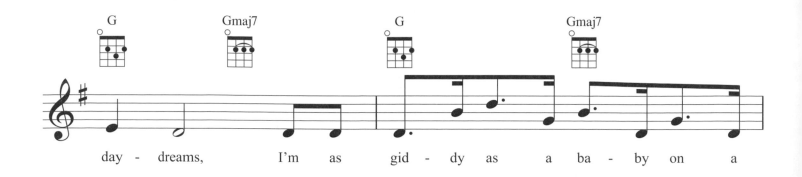

day - dreams, I'm as gid - dy as a ba - by on a

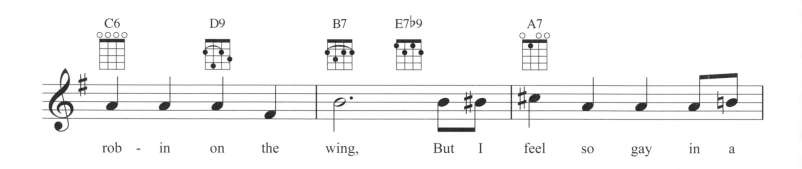

swing. I have - n't seen a cro - cus or a rose - bud, or a

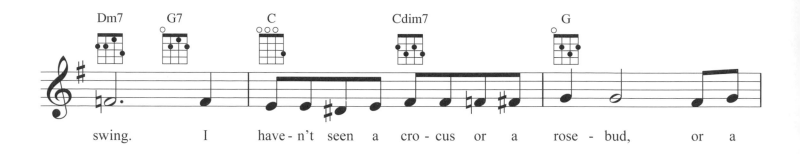

rob - in on the wing, But I feel so gay in a

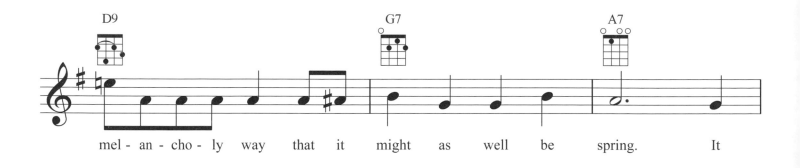

mel - an - cho - ly way that it might as well be spring. It

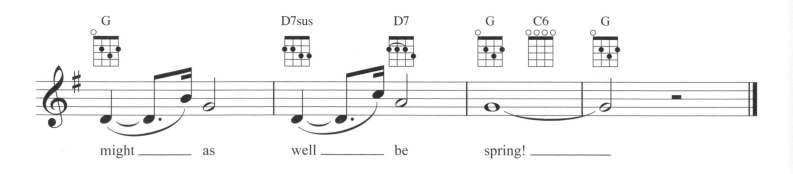

might _____ as well _____ be spring! _____

Imagine

Words and Music by John Lennon

Verse

2. I - mag - ine there's   no   coun - tries,
3. *See additional lyrics*

it   is - n't   hard ____   to   do; _____

noth - ing   to   kill   or   die _____   for

and   no   re - li - gion,   too. _____

I - mag - ine   all   the   peo - ple _____

liv - ing   life   in   peace. ____   You, _____

Chorus

Additional Lyrics

3. Imagine no possessions,
   I wonder if you can;
   No need for greed or hunger,
   A brotherhood of man.
   Imagine all the people sharing all the world.

Just the Way You Are

Words and Music by Billy Joel

The Lady Is a Tramp

from BABES IN ARMS
Words by Lorenz Hart
Music by Richard Rodgers

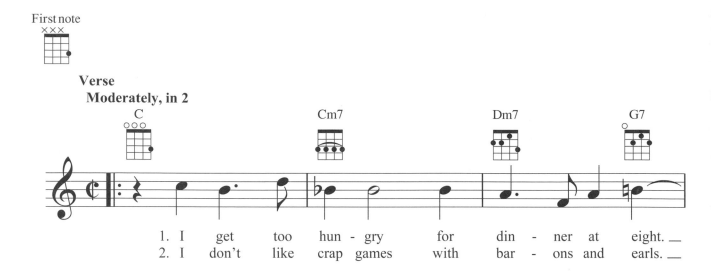

1. I get too hun - gry for din - ner at eight. __
2. I don't like crap games with bar - ons and earls. __

__ I like the thea - tre, but
__ Won't go to Har - lem in

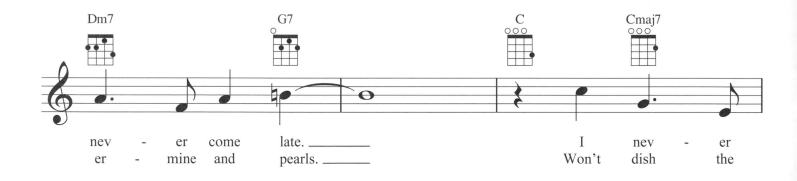

nev - er come late. _____ I nev - er
er - mine and pearls. _____ Won't dish the

both - er with peo - ple I hate. _____ }
dirt with the rest of the girls. _____ }

That's why the la - dy is a tramp.

Bridge

I like the free, fresh

wind in my hair, _____ life with - out care. _____

Outro-Verse

I'm broke, _ it's oke. _ Hate Cal - i -

for - nia; it's cold and it's damp. _____

That's why the la - dy is a tramp. _____

Let It Be

Words and Music by John Lennon and Paul McCartney

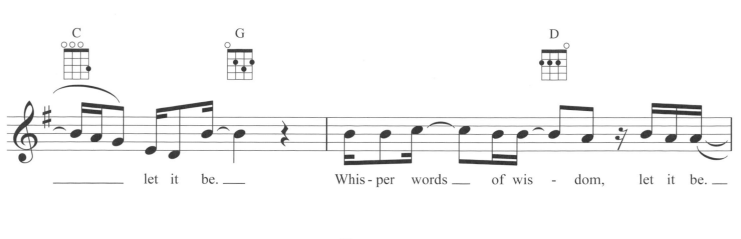

_____ let it be. ___ Whis - per words ___ of wis - dom, let it be. ___

Verse

_____ 2. And when the bro - ken - heart - ed peo - ple
3. And when the night ___ is cloud - y, there is

liv - ing in ___ the world a - gree, there will be an an - swer, let it
still a light ___ that shines on me, shine un - til to - mor - row, let it

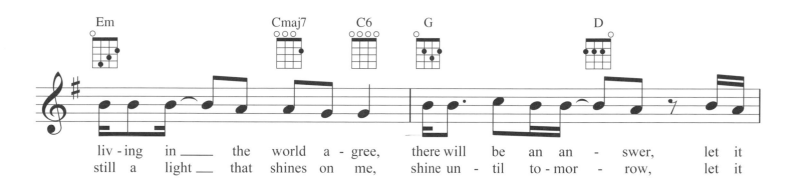

be. _____ For though they may be part - ed, there is
be. _____ I wake up to the sound ___ of mu - sic,

still a chance that they ___ will see, ___ there will be an an - swer, let it
Moth - er Mar - y comes ___ to me, ___ speak - ing words of wis - dom, let it

Chorus

be. _____
be. _____

Let it be, _____ let it be, _____ let it be, —

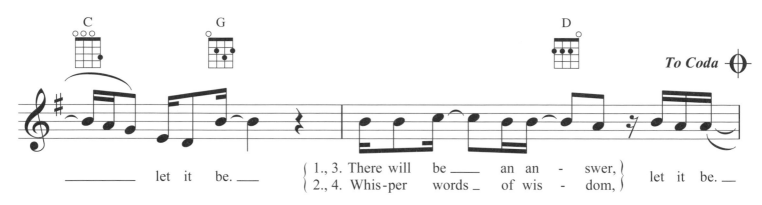

_____ let it be. —

{ 1., 3. There will be _____ an an - swer, }
{ 2., 4. Whis-per words _ of wis - dom, } let it be. —

To Coda ⊕

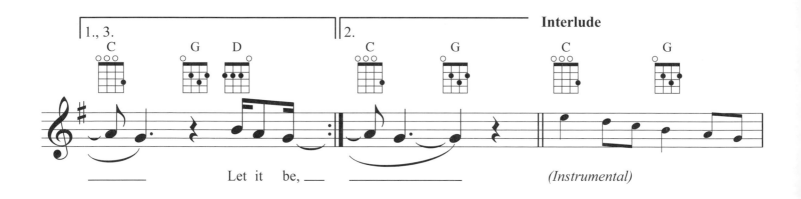

1., 3. | 2. **Interlude**

_____ Let it be, _____ _____ *(Instrumental)*

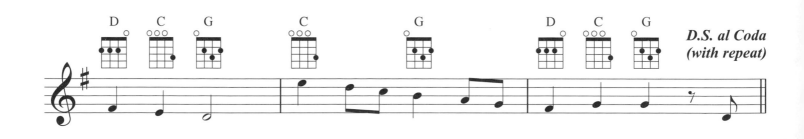

D.S. al Coda (with repeat)

⊕ **Coda**

_____ *(Instrumental)*

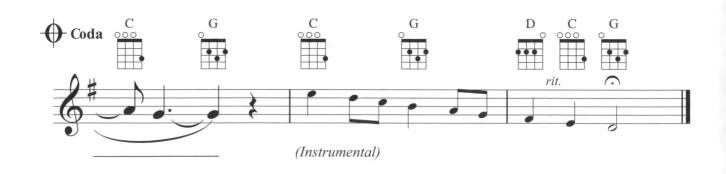

Love Me Tender

Words and Music by Elvis Presley and Vera Matson

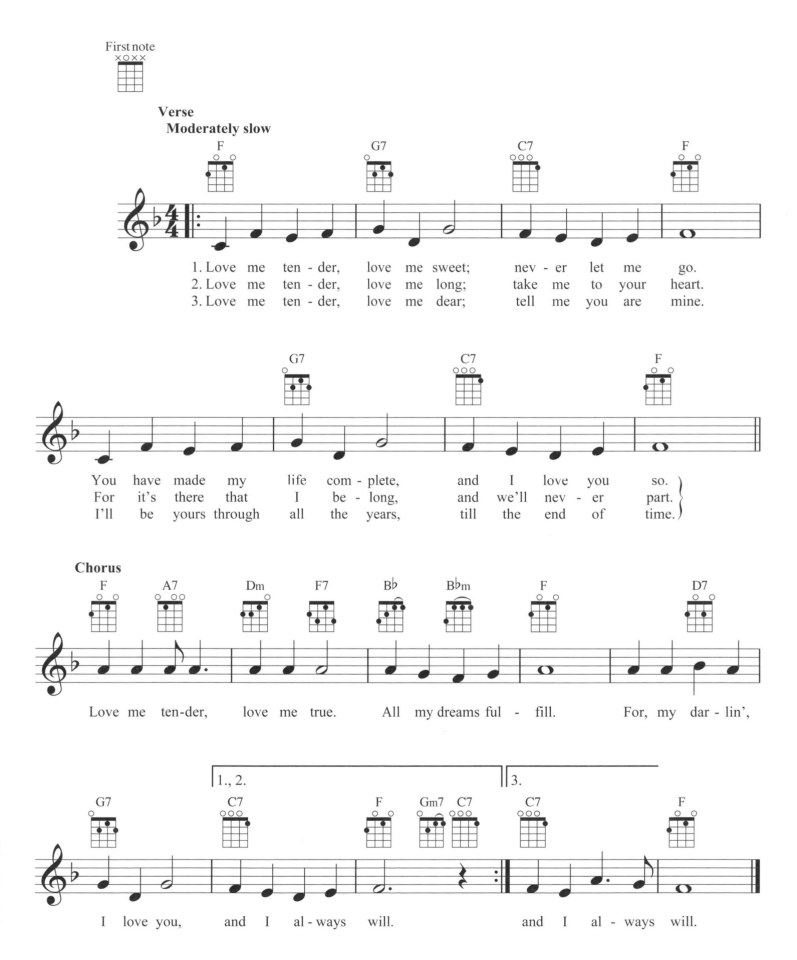

Let It Be Me

(Je t'appartiens)

English Words by Mann Curtis
French Words by Pierre Delanoe
Music by Gilbert Becaud

Verse
Moderately

1. I bless the day I found you, I want to
2. If for each bit of glad - ness, some - one must

stay a - round you, and so I beg you,
taste of sad - ness, I'll bear the sor - row,

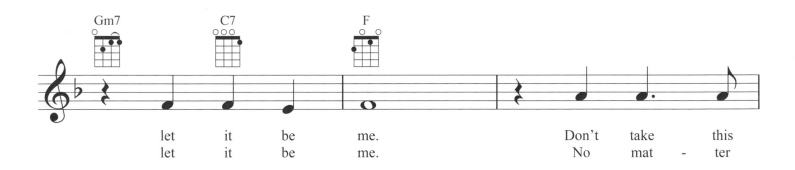

let it be me. Don't take this
let it be me. No mat - ter

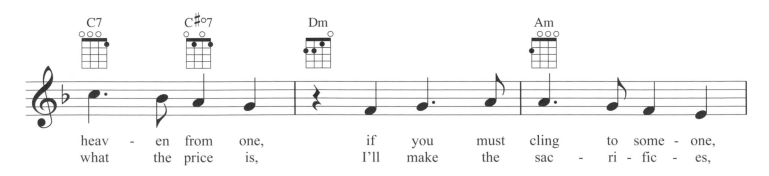

heav - en from one, if you must cling to some - one,
what the price is, I'll make the sac - ri - fic - es,

Love Walked In

from GOLDWYN FOLLIES

Music and Lyrics by George Gershwin and Ira Gershwin

Chorus

One look and I for - got the gloom of the

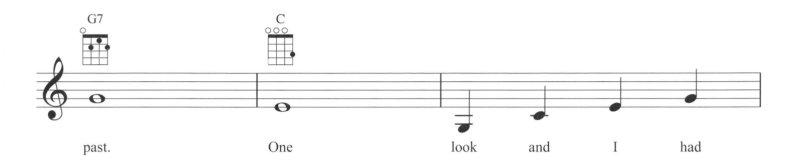

past. One look and I had

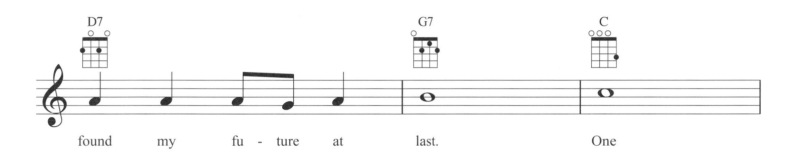

found my fu - ture at last. One

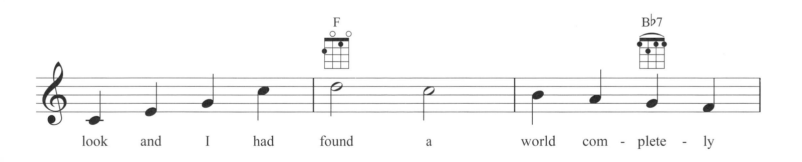

look and I had found a world com - plete - ly

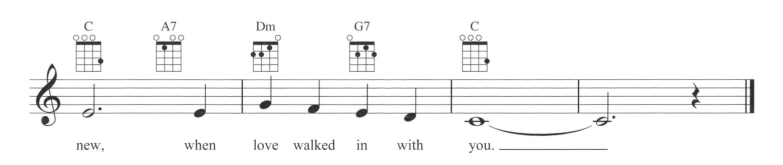

new, when love walked in with you. _____

Memory

from CATS
Music by Andrew Lloyd Webber
Text by Trevor Nunn after T.S. Eliot

fa - tal - is - tic warn - ing. Some - one mut - ters __ and a
stale, cold smell __ of morn - ing. The street lamp dies; an - oth - er

street lamp gut - ters, __ and soon it will be morn - ing.
night is o - ver, __ an - oth - er day is dawn - ing.

Verse

3. Day - light. _____ I must wait for the sun - rise. _____ I must think of a
4. Touch me. _____ It's so eas - y to leave me _____ all a - lone with the

new life _____ and I must - n't give in. _____ When the
mem - 'ry _____ of my days in the sun. _____ If you

dawn comes, to - night will be a mem - o - ry too, _____ and a
touch me, you'll un - der - stand what hap - pi - ness is. _____ Look, a

1.
2.

new day _____ will be - gin.
new day _____ has be - gun.

Moon River

from the Paramount Picture BREAKFAST AT TIFFANY'S
Words by Johnny Mercer
Music by Henry Mancini

First note

Chorus
Slowly

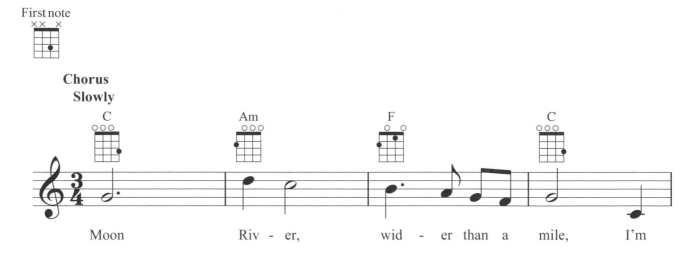

Moon Riv-er, wid-er than a mile, I'm

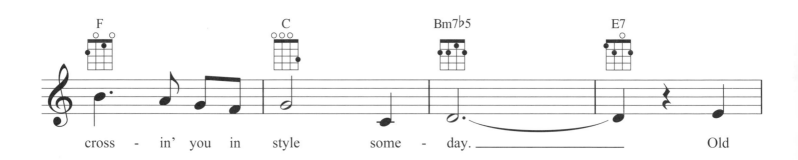

cross-in' you in style some-day. _____ Old

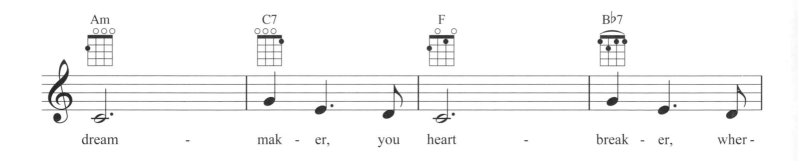

dream-mak-er, you heart-break-er, wher-

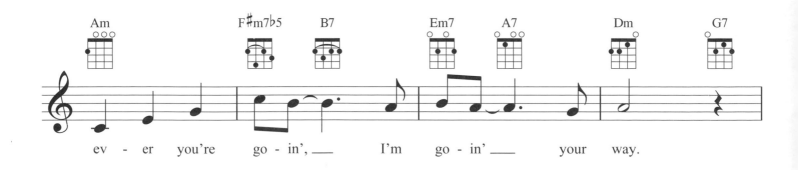

ev-er you're go-in', ___ I'm go-in' ___ your way.

Moonlight in Vermont

Words by John Blackburn
Music by Karl Suessdorf

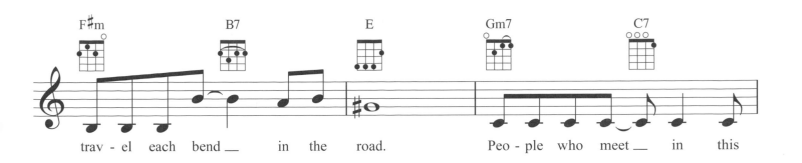

trav - el each bend ___ in the road. Peo - ple who meet ___ in this

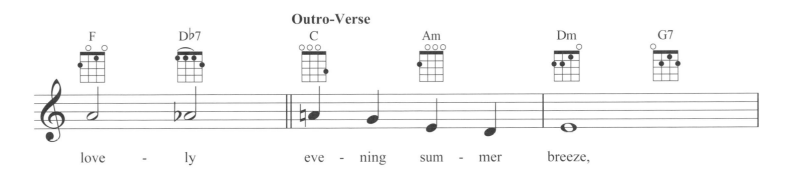

ro - man - tic set - ting are so hyp - no - tized ___ by the

Outro-Verse

love - ly eve - ning sum - mer breeze,

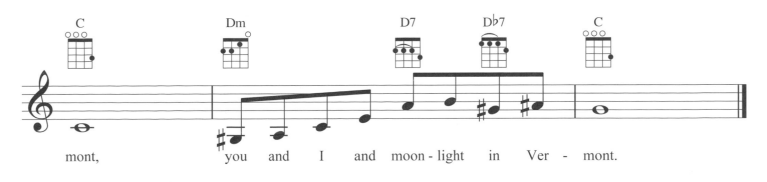

war - bling of a mead - ow - lark, moon - light in Ver -

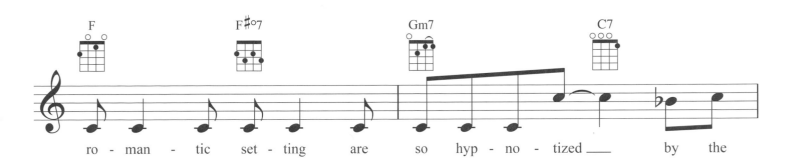

mont, you and I and moon - light in Ver - mont.

My Favorite Things

from THE SOUND OF MUSIC
Lyrics by Oscar Hammerstein II
Music by Richard Rodgers

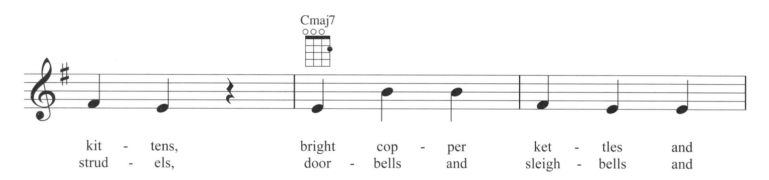

1. Rain - drops on ros - es and whisk - ers on
2. Cream - col - ored po - nies and crisp ap - ple

kit - tens, bright cop - per ket - tles and
strud - els, door - bells and sleigh - bells and

warm wool - en mit - tens, brown pa - per
schnitz - el with noo - dles, wild geese that

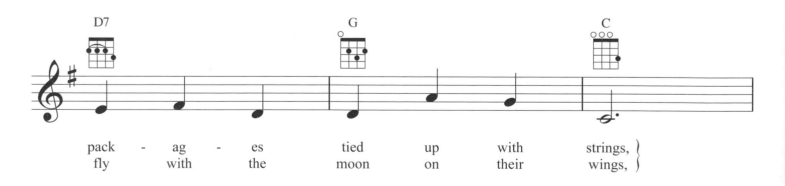

pack - ag - es tied up with strings, }
fly with the moon on their wings, }

these are a few of my fa - vor - ite things.

Outro

When the dog bites, when the bee stings,

when I'm feel - ing sad, _____ I

sim - ply re - mem - ber my fa - vor - ite

things and then I don't feel

so bad. _____

My Heart Will Go On
(Love Theme from 'Titanic')
from the Paramount and Twentieth Century Fox Motion Picture TITANIC
Music by James Horner
Lyric by Will Jennings

here; there's noth - ing I fear, ____ and I know ____

____ that my heart will go on. ____

____ We'll stay for -

ev - er this way. ____ You are safe in my

heart, and my heart will go on and on. ____

____ Mm. ____

My Funny Valentine

from BABES IN ARMS
Words by Lorenz Hart
Music by Richard Rodgers

My Way

English Words by Paul Anka
Original French Words by Gilles Thibault
Music by Jacques Revaux and Claude François

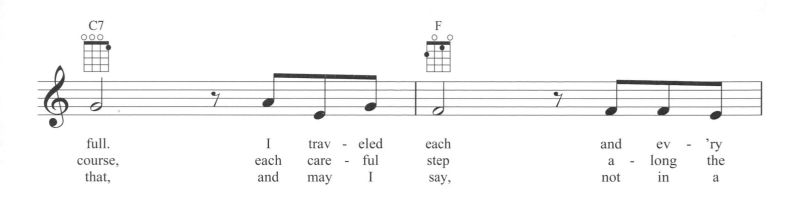

full. / course, / that,

I / each / and

trav - eled / care - ful / may I

each / step / say,

and / a - long / not in

ev - 'ry / the / a

high - way, / by - way, / shy way.

and / and / Oh,

more, / more, / no,

much more than / much more than / oh, no, not

this, / this, / me,

I / I / I

did / did / did

it / it / it

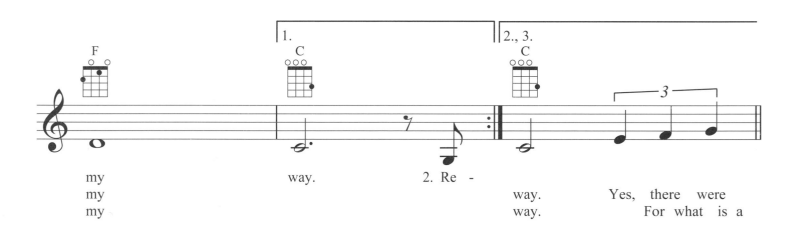

my / my / my

way.

2. Re -

way. / way.

Yes, there were / For what is a

Chorus

times, / man?

I'm sure you / What has he

knew, / got?

when I / If not

bit / him -

off / self, more / than than / then I / he could / has chew. / naught. But / To through / say it / the

all, / things when / he there tru - / was ly doubt, / feels, I / and ate not / it the

To Coda ⊕

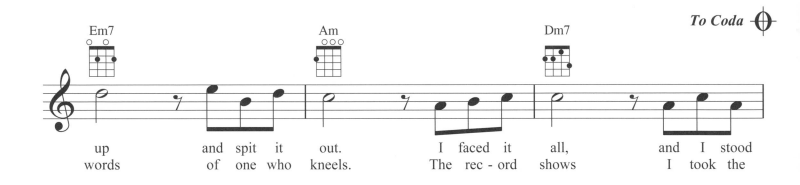

up / words and / of spit one / it who out. / kneels. I / The faced rec - / it ord all, / shows and / I I took / stood the

D.S. al Coda
(take 2nd ending)

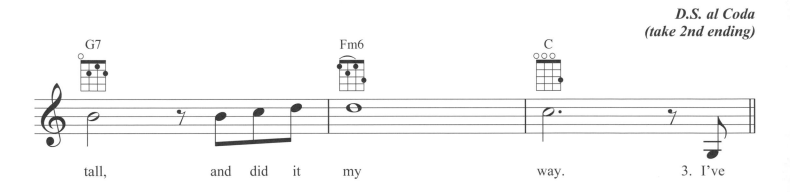

tall, and / did it / my way. 3. I've

⊕ **Coda**

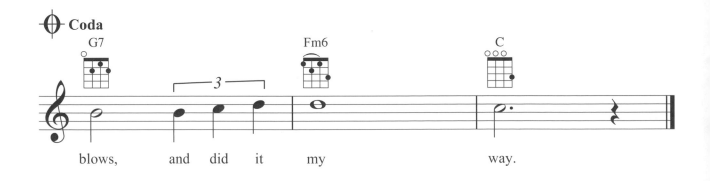

blows, and / did it / my way.

Night and Day

Words and Music by Cole Porter

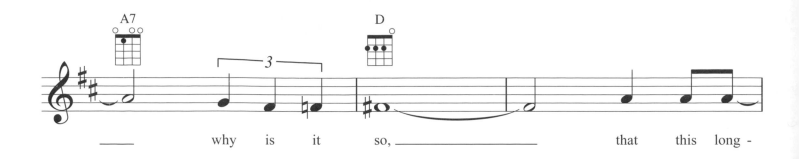

_____ why is it so, _____ that this long -

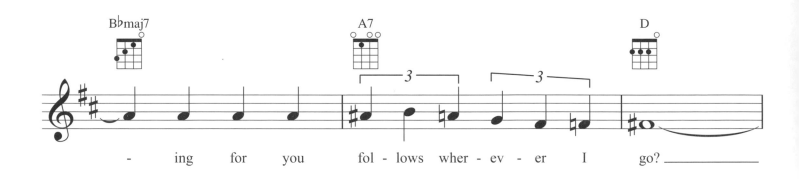

- ing for you fol - lows wher - ev - er I go? _____

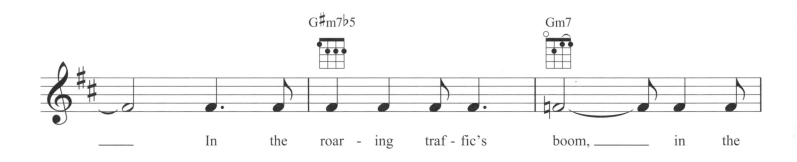

_____ In the roar - ing traf - fic's boom, _____ in the

si - lence of my lone - ly room, __ I think of you _____

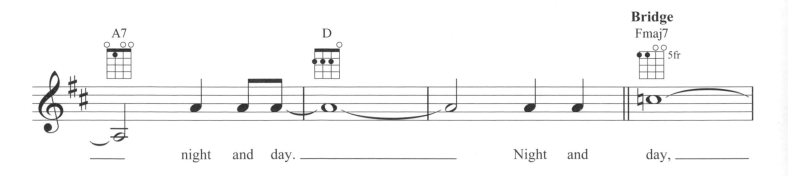

_____ night and day. _____ Night and day, _____

114

_____ un-der the hide of me, _____ there's an,

oh, such a hun-gry yearn - ing burn - ing in - side of me. _____

Outro

_____ And its tor - ment won't be through _____ 'til you

let me spend my life mak-ing love ___ to you, day and night, _____

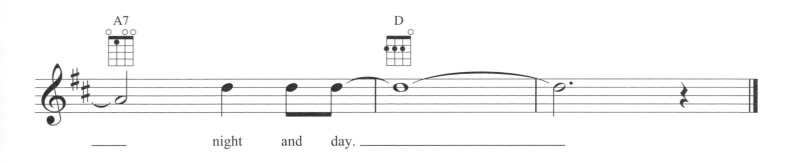

_____ night and day. _____

Over the Rainbow

from THE WIZARD OF OZ
Music by Harold Arlen
Lyric by E.Y. "Yip" Harburg

First note

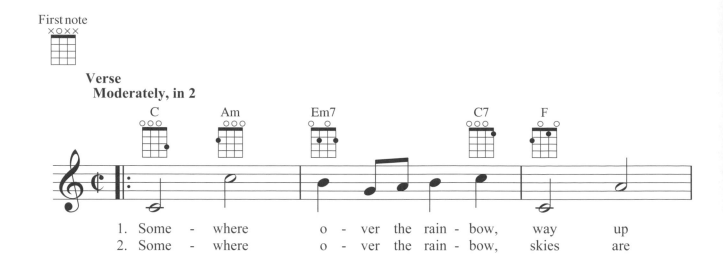

Verse
Moderately, in 2

1. Some - where o - ver the rain - bow, way up
2. Some - where o - ver the rain - bow, skies up are

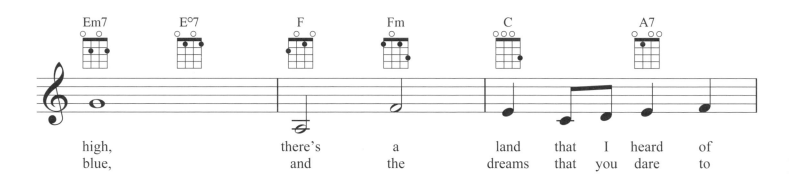

high, there's a land that I heard of
blue, and the dreams that you dare to

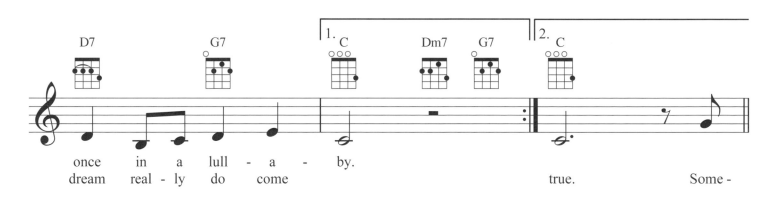

once in a lull - a - by.
dream real - ly do come true. Some -

Bridge

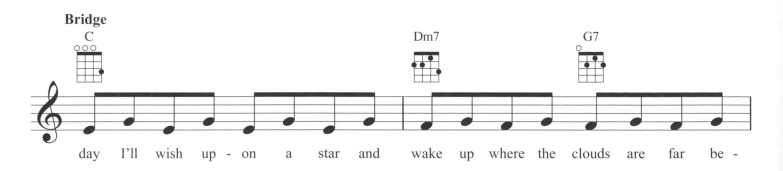

day I'll wish up - on a star and wake up where the clouds are far be -

Piano Man

Words and Music by Billy Joel

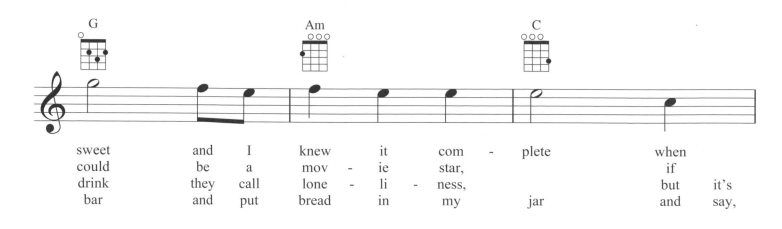

sweet and I knew it com - plete when
could be a mov - ie star, if
drink they call lone - li - ness, but it's
bar and put bread in my jar and say,

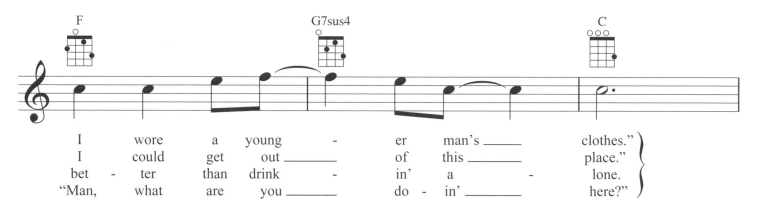

I wore a young - er man's _____ clothes."
I could get out _____ of this _____ place."
bet - ter than drink - in' a - lone.
"Man, what are you _____ do - in' _____ here?"

Pre-Chorus

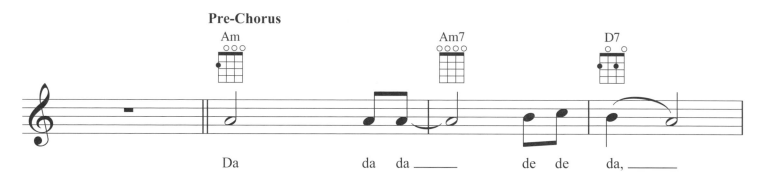

Da da da _____ de de da, _____

da da _____ de de da _____

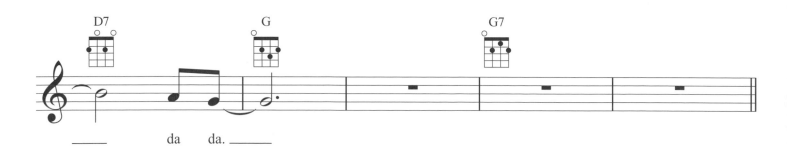

_____ da da. _____

Chorus

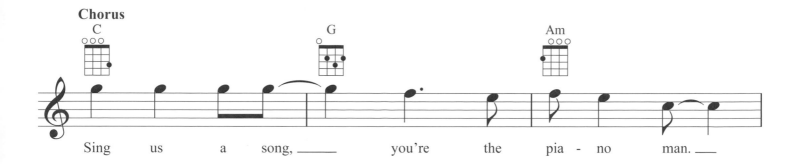

Sing us a song, _____ you're the pia - no man. ___

Sing us a song _____ to - night. ___

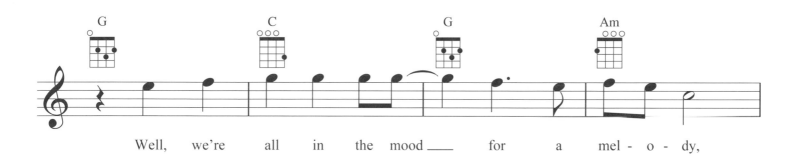

Well, we're all in the mood ___ for a mel - o - dy,

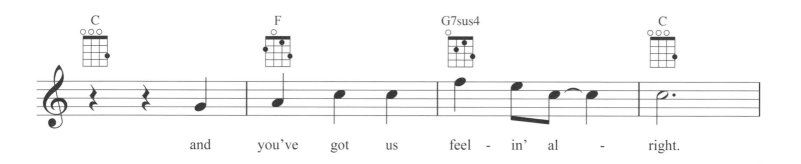

and you've got us feel - in' al - right.

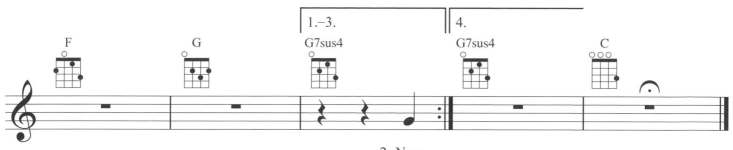

2. Now,
3. Now,
4. It's a

Satin Doll

By Duke Ellington

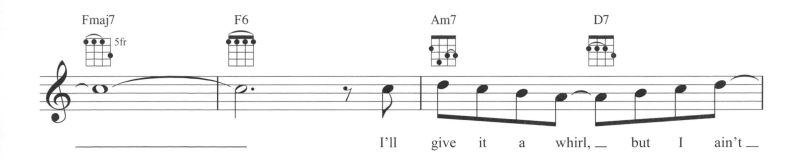

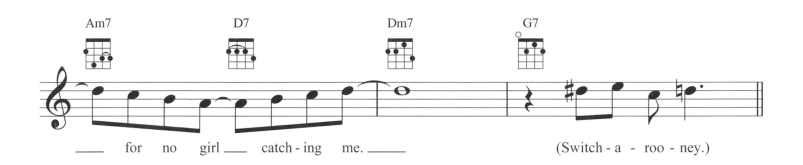

I'll give it a whirl, __ but I ain't __

__ for no girl __ catch - ing me. _____ (Switch - a - roo - ney.)

Outro

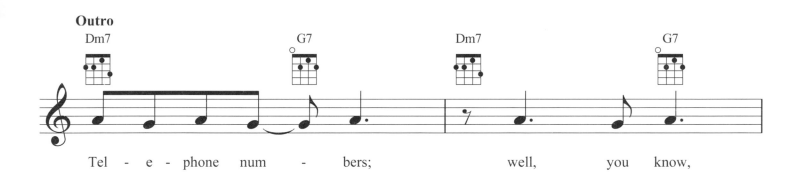

Tel - e - phone num - bers; well, you know,

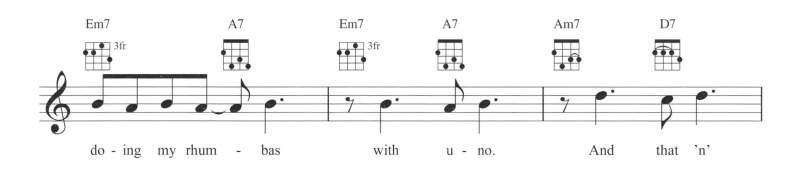

do - ing my rhum - bas with u - no. And that 'n'

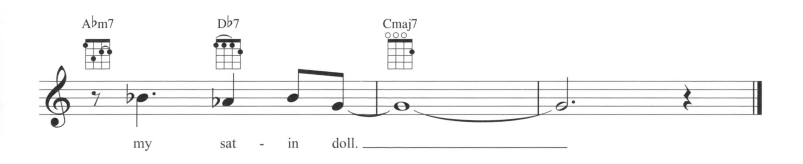

my sat - in doll. _____

Send in the Clowns

from the Musical A LITTLE NIGHT MUSIC
Words and Music by Stephen Sondheim

First note

Verse
Moderately slow, freely

1. Is-n't it rich?   Are we a pair?   Me here at
(2.) bliss?   Don't you ap - prove?   One who keeps

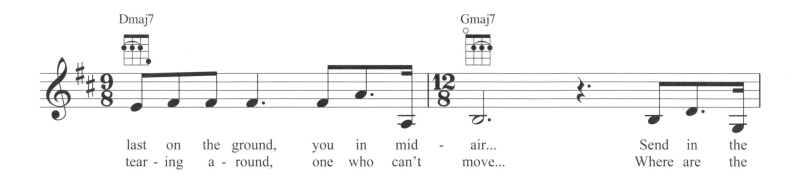

last on the ground,   you in mid - air...   Send in the
tear - ing a - round,   one who can't move...   Where are the

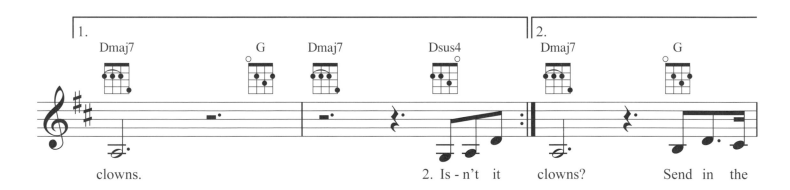

clowns.   2. Is - n't it clowns?   Send in the

Bridge

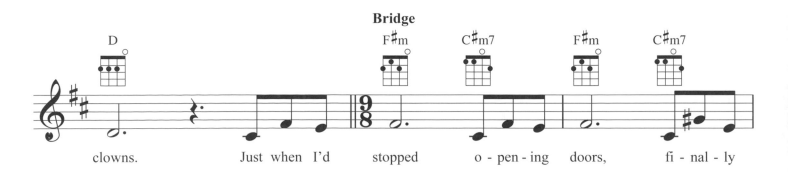

clowns.   Just when I'd stopped o - pen - ing doors,   fi - nal - ly

knowing the one that I wanted was yours, making my

en - trance a - gain with my u - su - al flair, sure of my

lines, no one is there. Is - n't it

Outro-Verse

rich? Is - n't it queer, los - ing my

tim - ing this late in my ca - reer? And where are the

rit.

clowns? Quick, send in the clowns. Don't both - er, they're here.

Skylark

Words by Johnny Mercer
Music by Hoagy Carmichael

Outro-Verse

127

Some Day My Prince Will Come

from SNOW WHITE AND THE SEVEN DWARFS
Words by Larry Morey
Music by Frank Churchill

First note
×× ×

Flowing

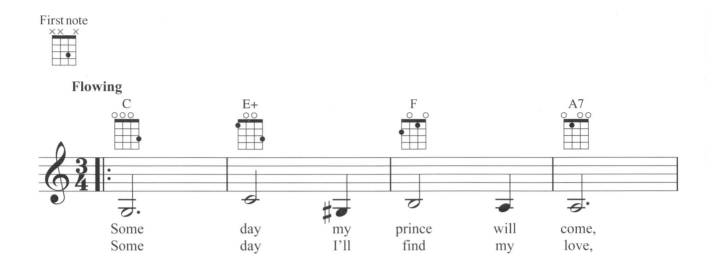

Some day my prince will come,
Some day I'll find my love,

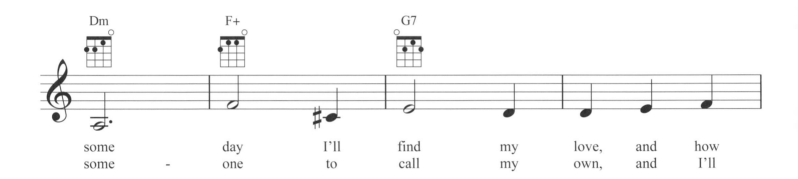

some day I'll find my love, and how
some - one to call my own, and I'll

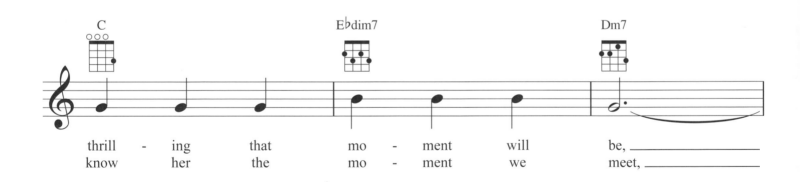

thrill - ing that mo - ment will be, _____
know her the mo - ment we meet, _____

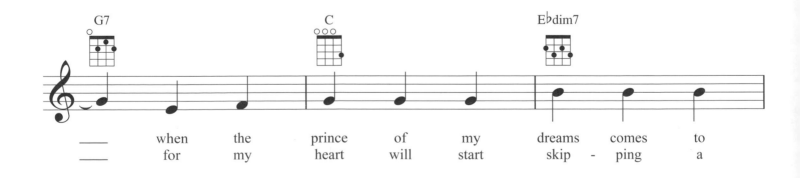

_____ when the prince of my dreams comes to
_____ for my prince heart of will my start dreams skip - comes ping to a

Someone to Watch Over Me

Music and Lyrics by George Gershwin and Ira Gershwin

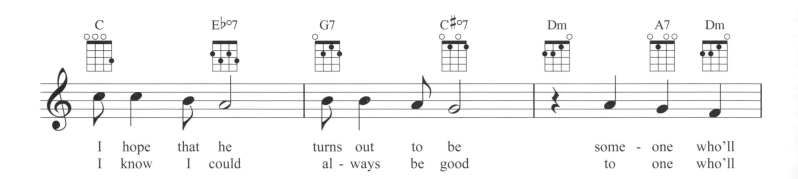

1. There's a some-bod-y I'm long-ing to see.
2. I'm a lit-tle lamb who's lost in the wood.

I hope that he turns out to be some-one who'll
I know I could turns al-ways be good to one who'll

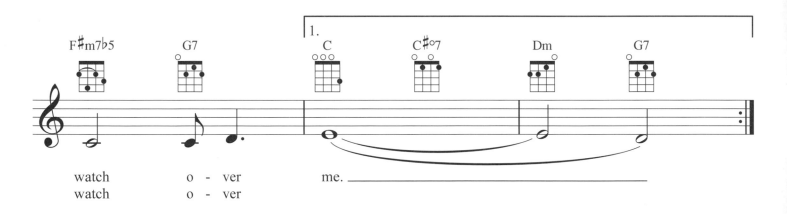

watch o-ver me.
watch o-ver

me. Al - though he may not be the

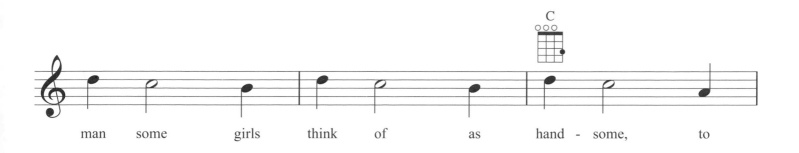

man some girls think of as hand - some, to

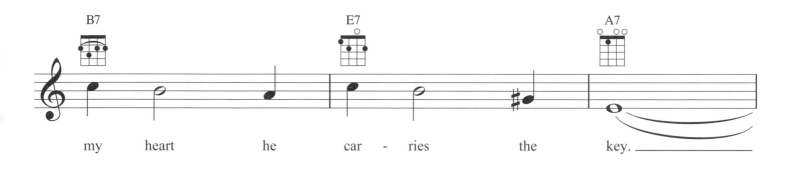

my heart he car - ries the key. ___

Outro-Verse

___ Won't you tell him, please, to put on some speed,

fol - low my lead? Oh, how I need some - one to

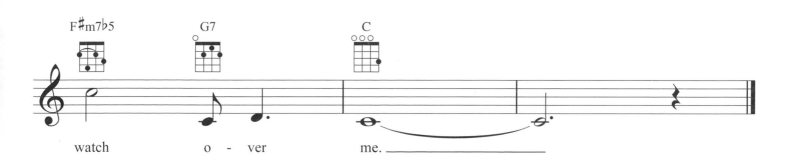

watch o - ver me. ___

Somewhere

from WEST SIDE STORY
Lyrics by Stephen Sondheim
Music by Leonard Bernstein

Outro-Verse

some-where. _____ There's a

place for us, a time and place for us.

Hold my hand and we're half - way there. Hold my hand and I'll

take you there, some - how, _____ some - day, _____

some - where. _____

Stormy Weather
(Keeps Rainin' All the Time)

from COTTON CLUB PARADE OF 1933
Lyric by Ted Koehler
Music by Harold Arlen

Bridge

time. _____ When he went a-way, the blues walked in and met me.

If he stays a-way, old rock-in' chair will get me. All I do is pray the Lord a-

bove will let me walk in the sun once more. Can't go

Outro-Verse

on; ev-'ry-thing I had is gone, storm-y weath-er. _____

Since my man and I ain't to-geth-er, _____ keeps rain-in' all the

time, _____ keeps rain-in' all the time. _____

Summertime

from PORGY AND BESS®

Music and Lyrics by George Gershwin, DuBose and Dorothy Heyward and Ira Gershwin

Tears in Heaven

Words and Music by Eric Clapton and Will Jennings

First note

Verse
Moderate, relaxed tempo

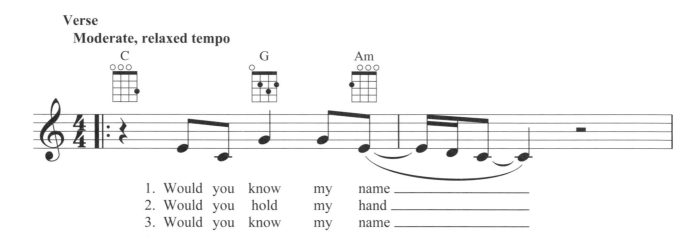

1. Would you know my name _____
2. Would you hold my hand _____
3. Would you know my name _____

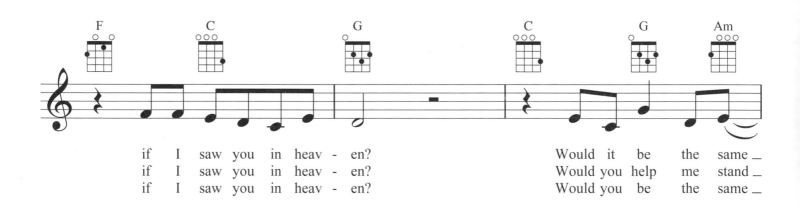

if I saw you in heav - en?   Would it be the same _
if I saw you in heav - en?   Would you help me stand _
if I saw you in heav - en?   Would you be the same _

_____   if I saw you in heav - en?
_____   if I saw you in heav - en?
_____   if I saw you in heav - en?

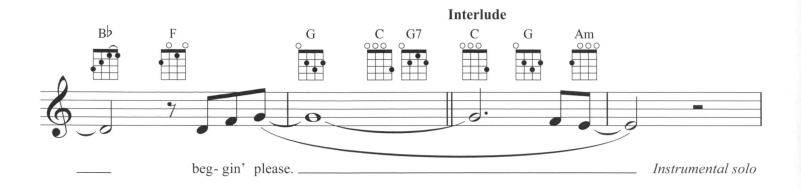

Interlude

_____ beg- gin' please. _____ *Instrumental solo*

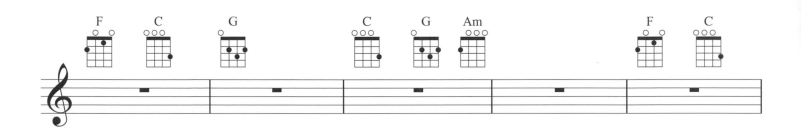

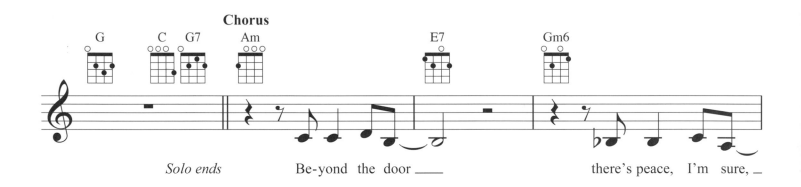

Chorus

Solo ends   Be-yond the door _____   there's peace, I'm sure, _

_____ and I know _ there'll be no more _____ tears in heav - en. *Instrumental solo*

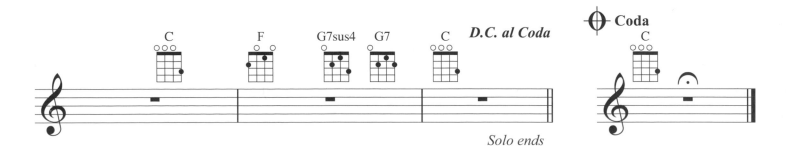

Solo ends

140

Stardust

Words by Mitchell Parish
Music by Hoagy Carmichael

First note

Verse
Moderately

1. And now the pur - ple dusk of twi - light time

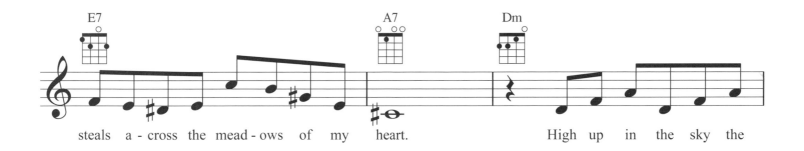

steals a - cross the mead - ows of my heart. High up in the sky the

lit - tle stars climb, al - ways re - mind - ing me that we're a - part.

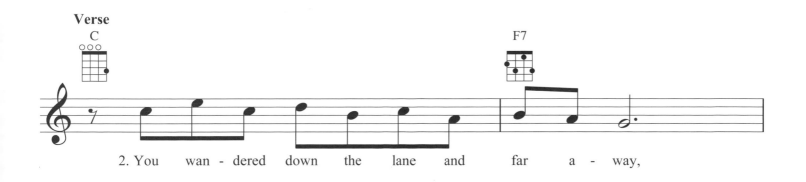

Verse

2. You wan - dered down the lane and far a - way,

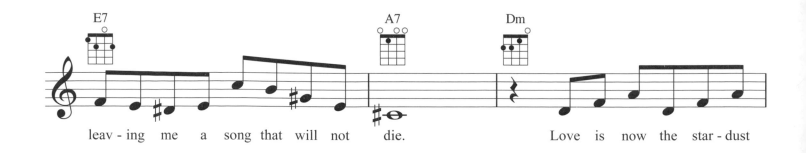

leav - ing me a song that will not die. Love is now the star - dust

of yes - ter - day, the mu - sic of the years gone by. _____ Some - times I

𝄋 Chorus

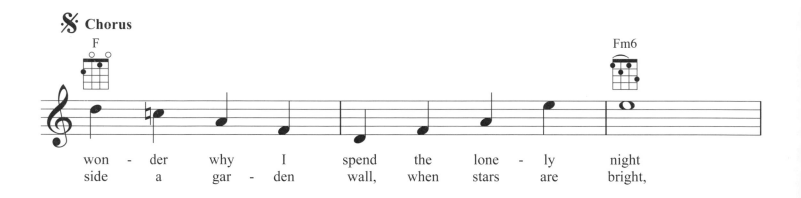

won - der why I spend the lone - ly night
side a gar - den wall, when stars are night bright,

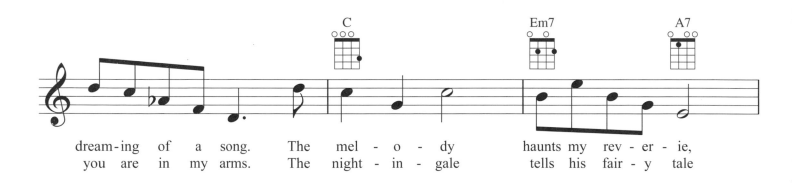

dream - ing of a song. The mel - o - dy haunts my rev - er - ie,
you are in my arms. The night - in - gale tells his fair - y tale

To Coda ⊕

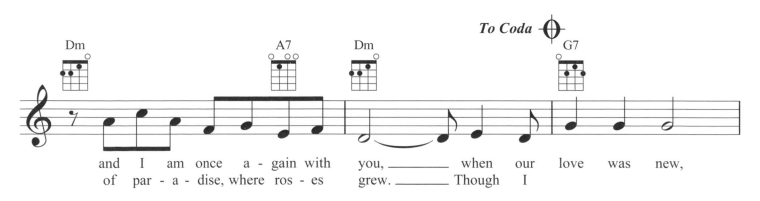

and I am once a - gain with you, _____ when our love was new,
of par - a - dise, where ros - es grew. _____ Though I

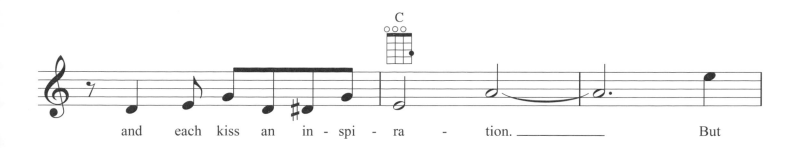

and each kiss an in - spi - ra - tion. _____ But

that was long a - go; now my con -so- la - tion is in the star -dust of a

D.S. al Coda   **Coda**

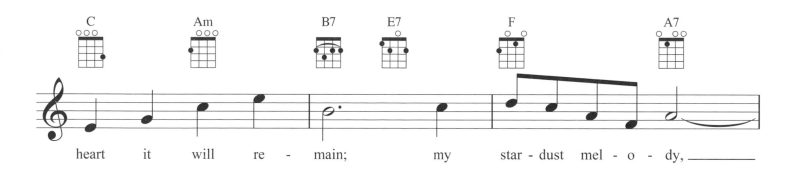

song. Be - dream in vain, _____ in my

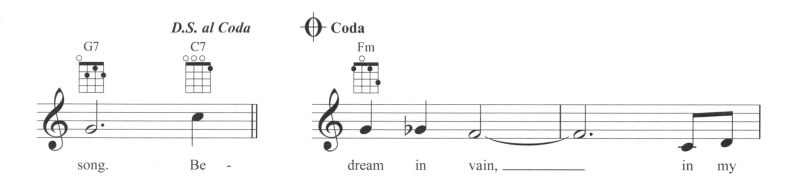

heart it will re - main; my star -dust mel - o - dy, _____

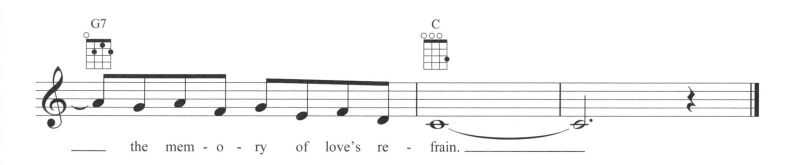

____ the mem - o - ry of love's re - frain. _____

They Can't Take That Away from Me

Music and Lyrics by George Gershwin and Ira Gershwin

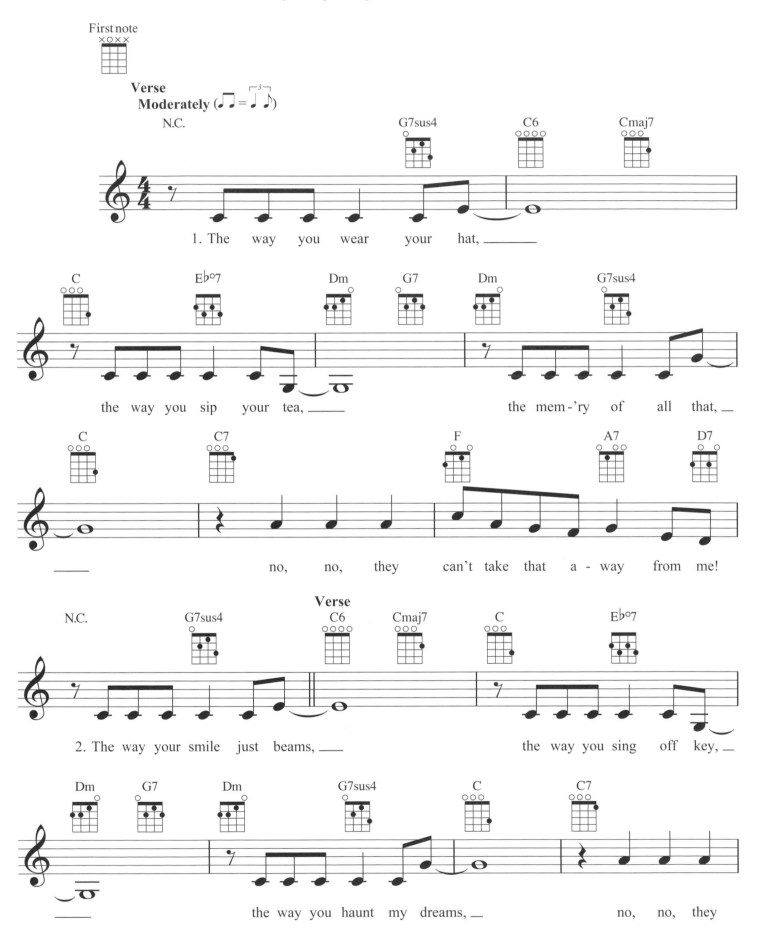

Bridge

F G7 C   Em B7

can't take that a - way from me! _____ We may nev - er, nev - er

Em A7 B7 Em F#7 F#m B7 Em B7

meet a - gain on the bump - y road to love, still I'll al - ways, al - ways

Em A7 D7 G7   **Outro-Verse**

               C6 Cmaj7

keep the mem - 'ry of the way you hold your knife, _____

C Eb°7 Dm G7 Dm G7sus4

the way we danced till three, _____ the way you've changed my life. _

C7   F G7 Am Dm7b5

_____ No, no! They can't take that a - way from me! No! They

C   Dm G7 C

can't take that a - way from me! _____

145

Top of the World

Words and Music by John Bettis and Richard Carpenter

First note

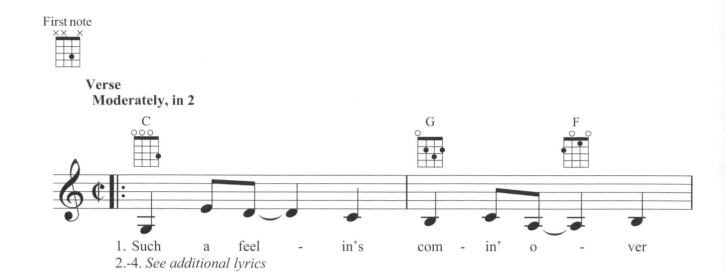

Verse
Moderately, in 2

1. Such a feel - in's com - in' o - ver
2.-4. *See additional lyrics*

me, _____ there is won - der in ___ most

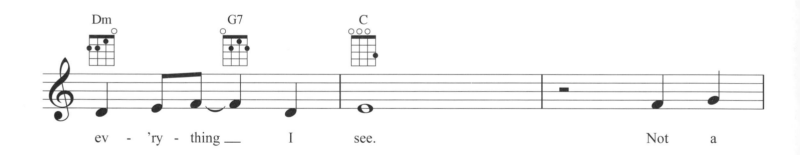

ev - 'ry - thing ___ I see. Not a

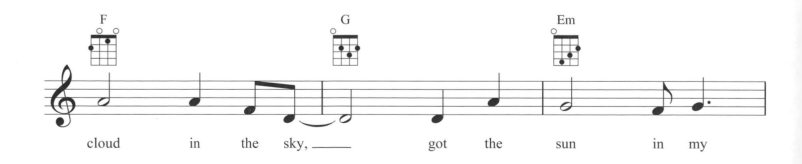

cloud in the sky, _____ got the sun in my

eyes, and I won't be sur - prised ____ if it's a

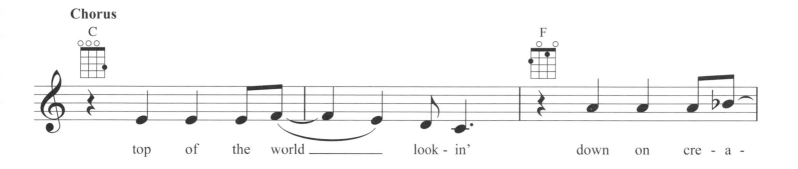

dream. _____ seen. I'm on the

Chorus

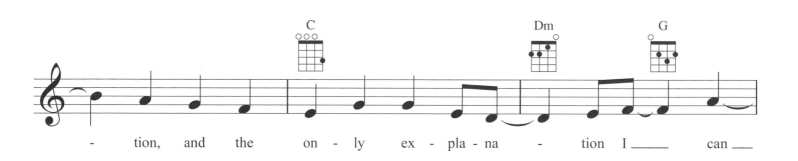

top of the world _____ look - in' down on cre - a -

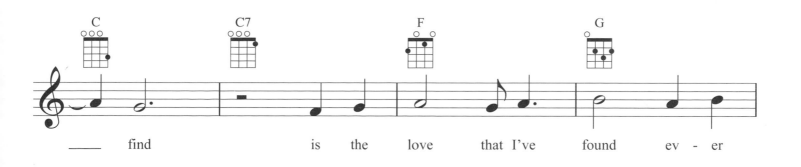

- tion, and the on - ly ex - pla - na - tion I ____ can ____

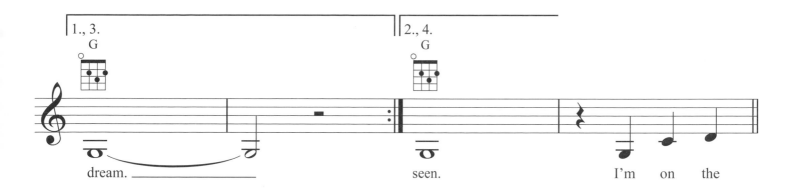

____ find is the love that I've found ev - er

147

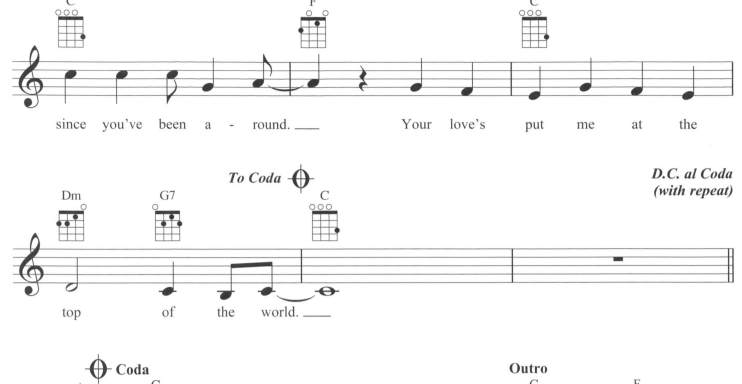

since you've been a - round. ____ Your love's put me at the

top of the world. ____

(Instrumental)

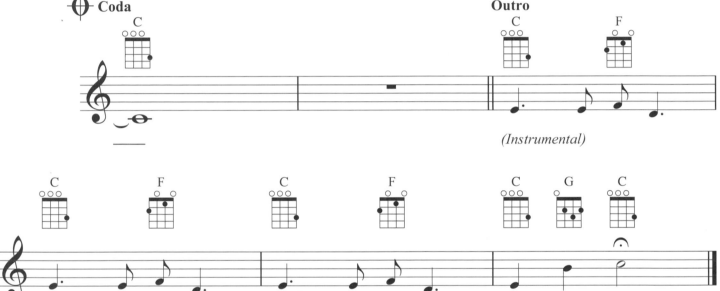

Additional Lyrics

2. Everything I want the world to be
   Is now coming true especially for me.
   And the reason is clear; it's because you are here.
   You're the nearest thing to heaven that I've seen.

3. Something in the wind has learned my name,
   And it's telling me that things are not the same.
   In the leaves on the trees and the touch of the breeze,
   There's a pleasing sense of happiness for me.

4. There is only one wish on my mind:
   When this day is through, I hope that I will find
   That tomorrow will be just the same for you and me.
   All I need will be mine if you are here.

What a Wonderful World

Words and Music by George David Weiss and Bob Thiele

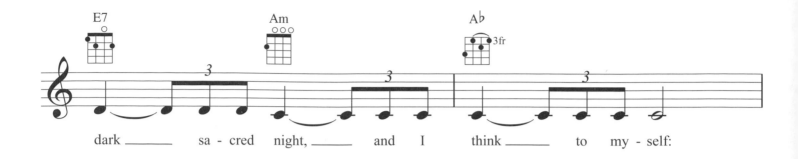

dark _____ sa - cred night, _____ and I think _____ to my - self:

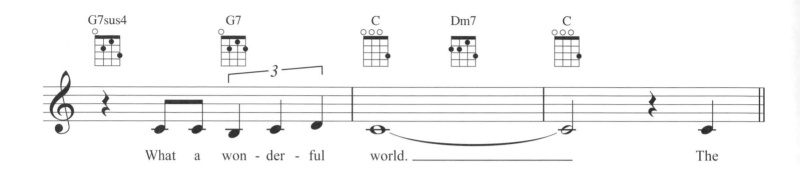

What a won - der - ful world. _____ The

Bridge

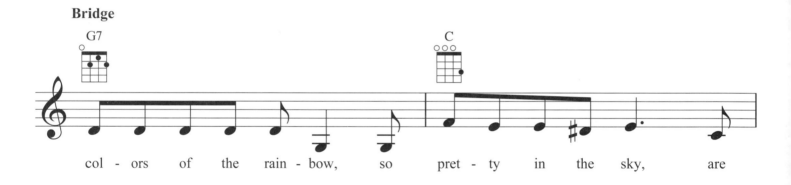

col - ors of the rain - bow, so pret - ty in the sky, are

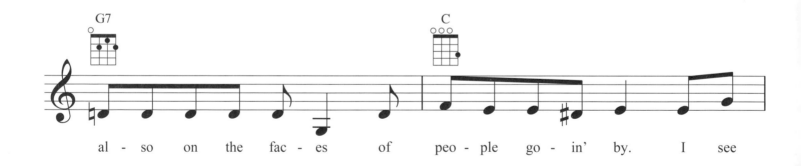

al - so on the fac - es of peo - ple go - in' by. I see

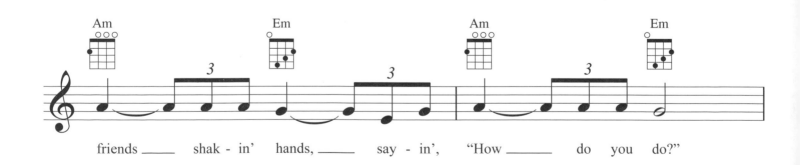

friends _____ shak - in' hands, _____ say - in', "How _____ do you do?"

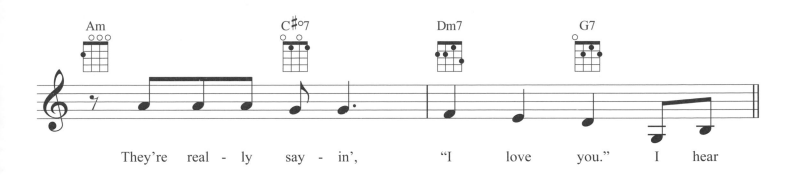

They're real - ly say - in', "I love you." I hear

Outro-Verse

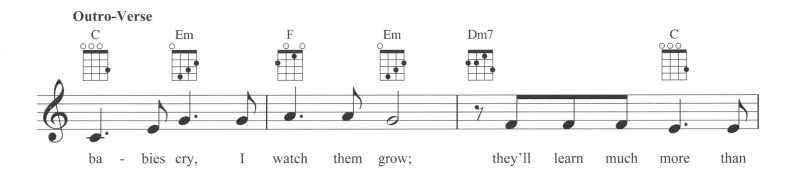

ba - bies cry, I watch them grow; they'll learn much more than

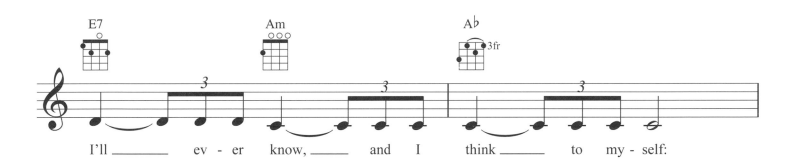

I'll _____ ev - er know, _____ and I think _____ to my - self:

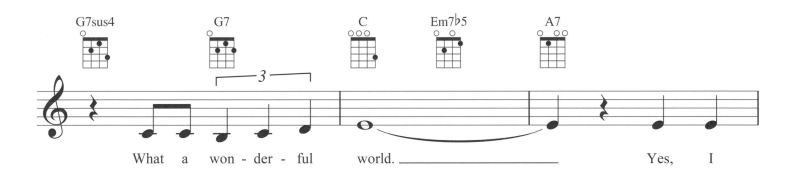

What a won - der - ful world. _____ Yes, I

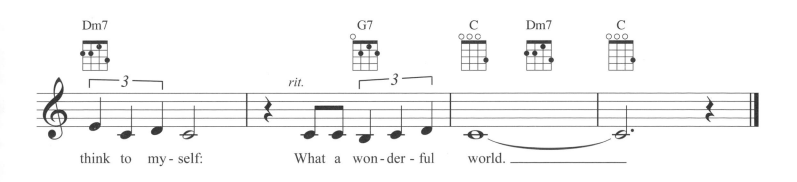

think to my - self: What a won - der - ful world. _____

Unchained Melody

Lyric by Hy Zaret
Music by Alex North

First note

Verse
Moderately slow

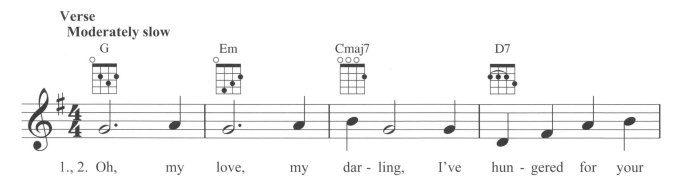

1., 2. Oh, my love, my dar - ling, I've hun - gered for your

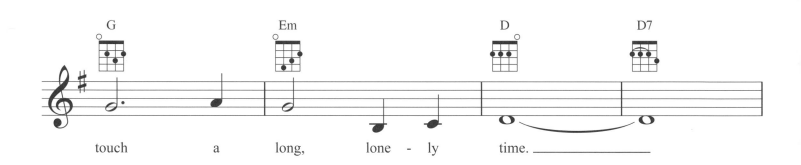

touch a long, lone - ly time. _____

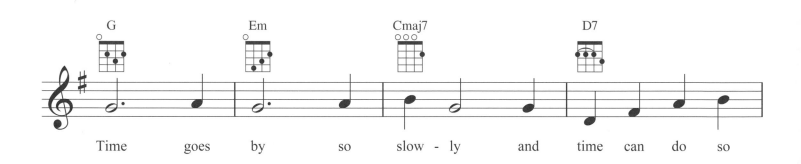

Time goes by so slow - ly and time can do so

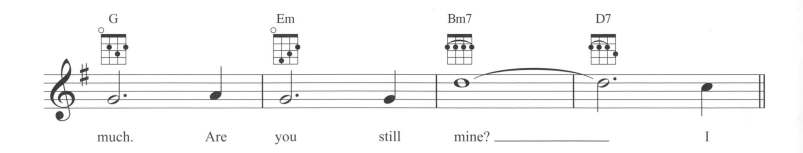

much. Are you still mine? _____ I

Unforgettable

Words and Music by Irving Gordon

First note

Chorus
Moderately

Un - for - get - ta - ble, _____ that's what you are. _____

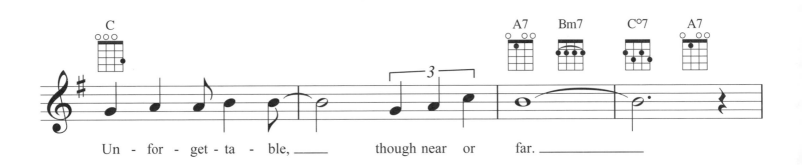

Un - for - get - ta - ble, _____ though near or far. _____

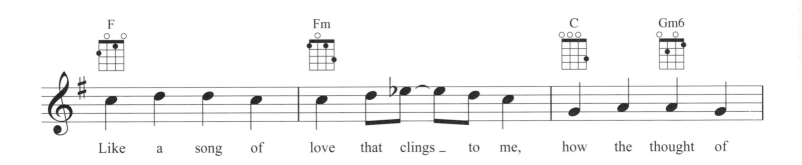

Like a song of love that clings _ to me, how the thought of

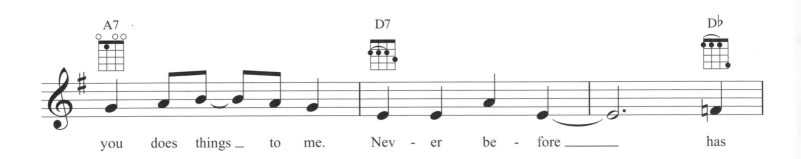

you does things _ to me. Nev - er be - fore _____ has

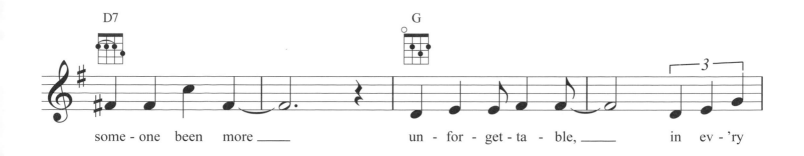

some - one been more _____ un - for - get - ta - ble, _____ in ev - 'ry

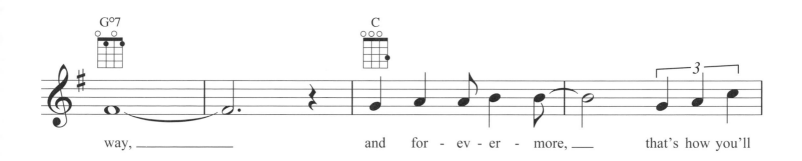

way, _____ and for - ev - er - more, ___ that's how you'll

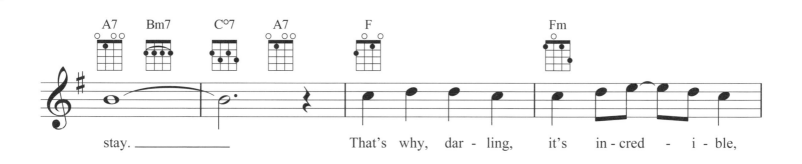

stay. _____ That's why, dar - ling, it's in - cred - i - ble,

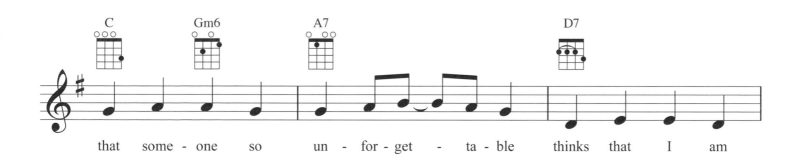

that some - one so un - for - get - ta - ble thinks that I am

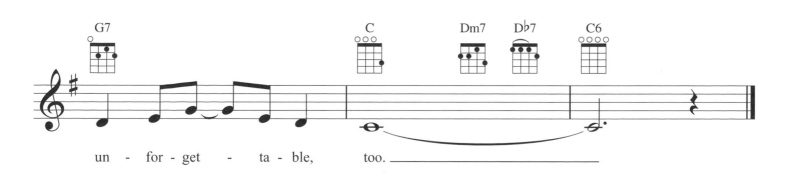

un - for - get - ta - ble, too. _____

The Very Thought of You

Words and Music by Ray Noble

We've Only Just Begun

Words and Music by Roger Nichols and Paul Williams

What Is This Thing Called Love?

Words and Music by Cole Porter

When I Fall in Love

Words by Edward Heyman
Music by Victor Young

Chorus

sun. When I give my heart, it will be com -

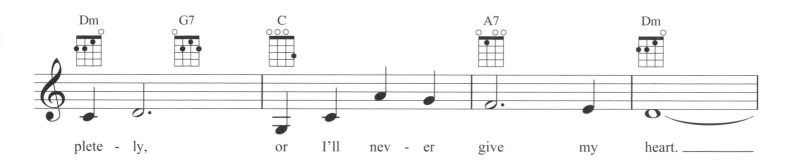

plete - ly, or I'll nev - er give my heart. _____

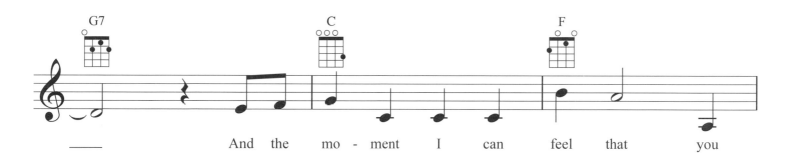

_____ And the mo - ment I can feel that you

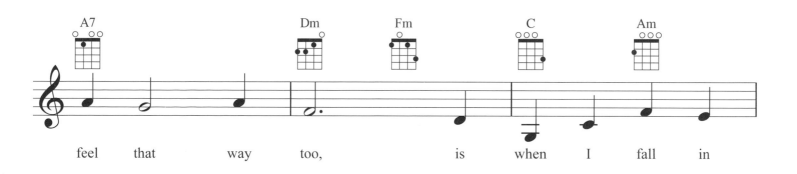

feel that way too, is when I fall in

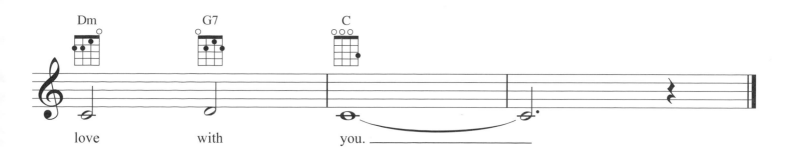

love with you. _____

When You Wish Upon a Star

from PINOCCHIO
Words by Ned Washington
Music by Leigh Harline

Chorus
Slowly, in 2

When you wish up - on a star,
If your heart is in your dream,

makes no dif - f'rence who you are,
no re - quest is too ex - treme,

an - y - thing your heart de - sires will
when you wish up - on a star as

1.
come to you.
dream - ers

2.
do.

Bridge

Fate is kind, she brings to

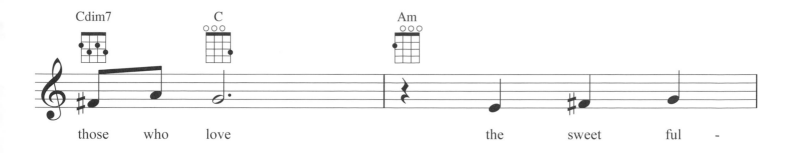

those who love the sweet ful -

fill - ment of their se - cret long -

Chorus

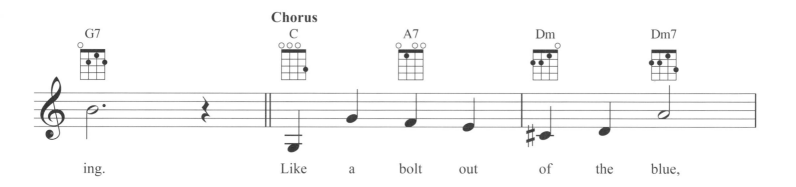

ing. Like a bolt out of the blue,

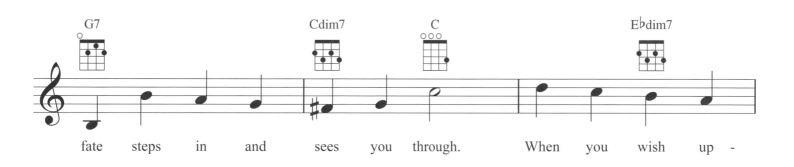

fate steps in and sees you through. When you wish up -

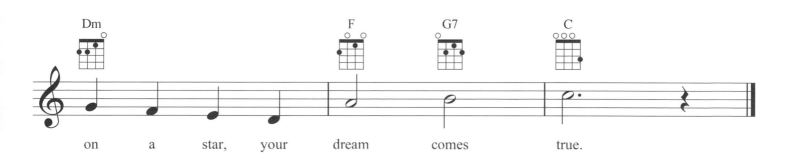

on a star, your dream comes true.

Yesterday

Words and Music by John Lennon and Paul McCartney

First note

Verse
Moderately, with expression

1. Yes - ter - day, ___ all my trou - bles seemed so
2. Sud - den - ly, ___ I'm not half the man I

far a - way. ___ Now it looks as though they're
used to be. ___ There's a shad - ow hang - ing

here to stay. ___ Oh, I be - lieve ___ in
o - ver me. ___ Oh, yes - ter - day ___ came

Bridge

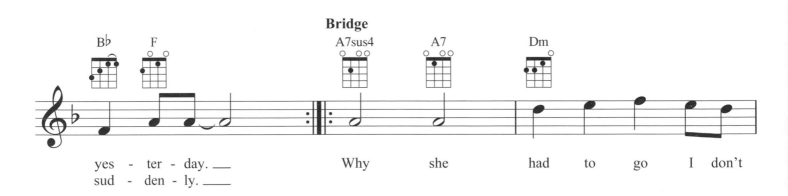

yes - ter - day. ___ Why she had to go I don't
sud - den - ly. ___

You Are So Beautiful

Words and Music by Billy Preston and Bruce Fisher

You Raise Me Up

Words and Music by Brendan Graham and Rolf Lovland

First note

Verse
Moderately slow

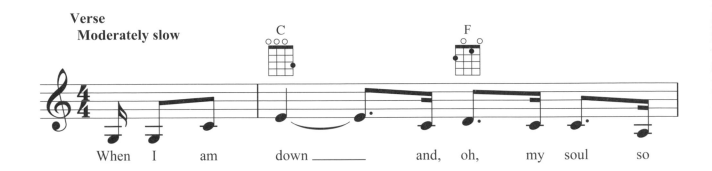

When I am down _____ and, oh, my soul so

wea - ry, when trou - bles come and my heart ___ bur - dened

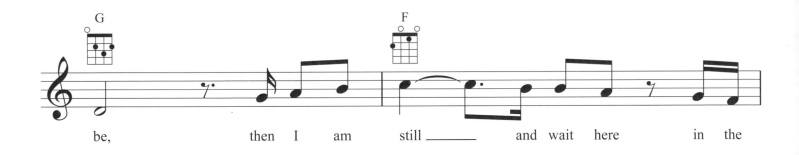

be, then I am still _____ and wait here in the

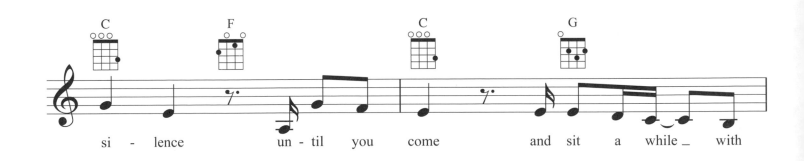

si - lence un - til you come and sit a while ___ with

Chorus

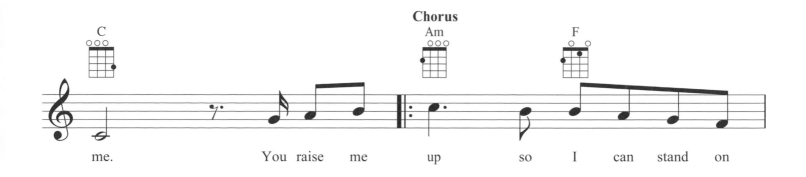

me.   You raise me up so I can stand on

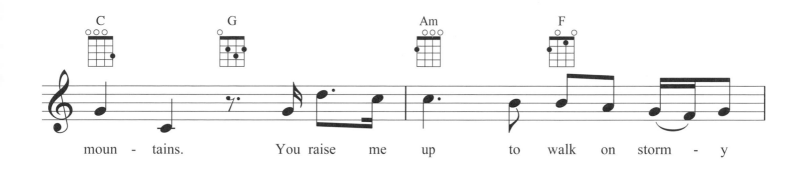

moun - tains.   You raise me up to walk on storm - y

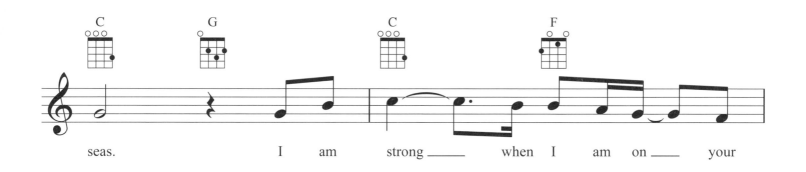

seas.   I am strong _____ when I am on _____ your

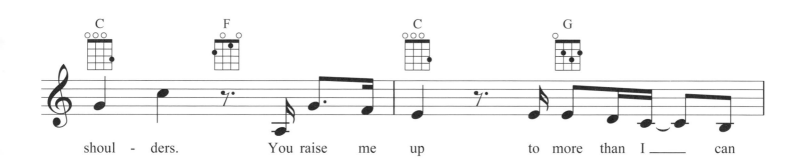

shoul - ders.   You raise me up to more than I _____ can

be.   You raise me   be.

You've Got a Friend in Me

from TOY STORY
Music and Lyrics by Randy Newman

You Are the Sunshine of My Life

Words and Music by Stevie Wonder

First note

Chorus
Moderately fast

You are the sun - shine of ___ my life.

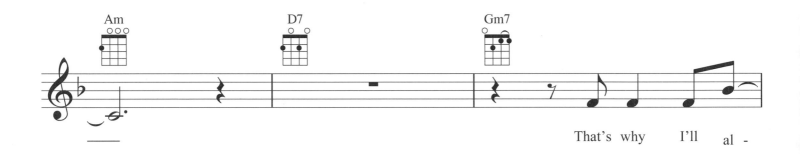

That's why I'll al -

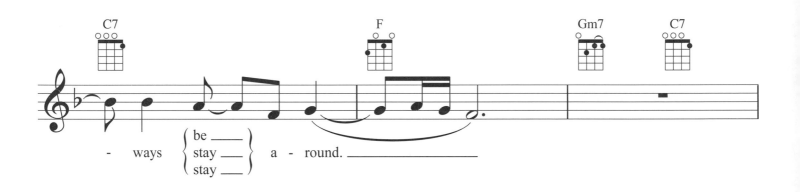

- ways { be ___ / stay ___ / stay ___ } a - round. _____

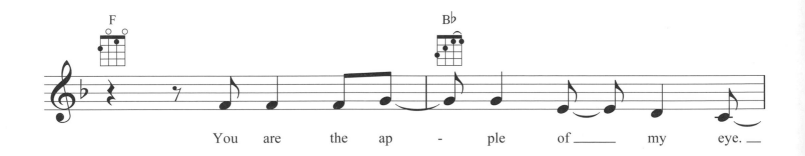

You are the ap - ple of ___ my eye. ___

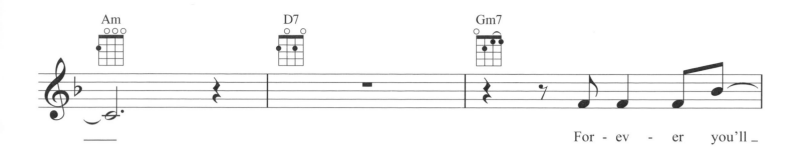

For - ev - er you'll _

To Coda ⊕

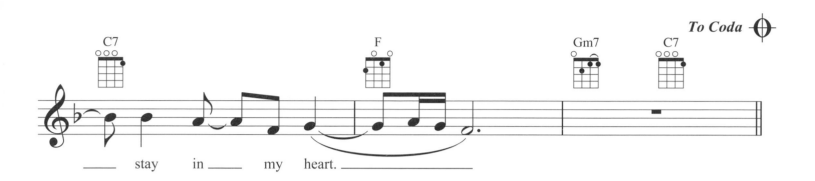

_____ stay in _____ my heart. _____

Verse

1. I feel like this _____ is the _____ be -
2. You must have known _____ that I _____ was _____

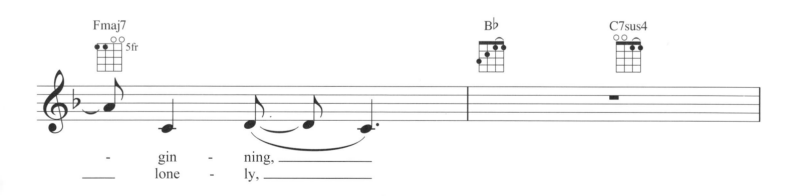

- gin - ning, _____
_____ lone - ly, _____

'though I've loved you _____ for a mil - lion years. _____
be - cause you came _____ to my _____ res - cue. _____

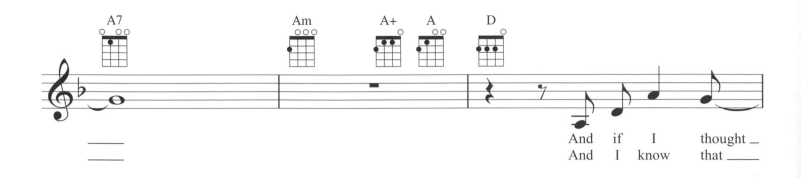

And if I thought ___
And I know that ___

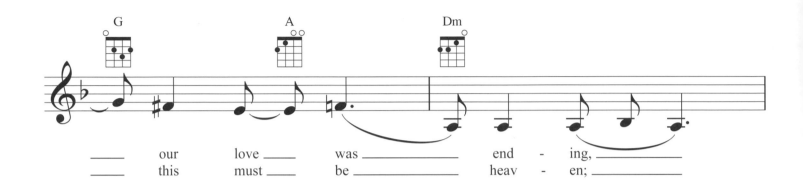

___ our love ___ was ___ end - ing, ___
___ this must ___ be ___ heav - en; ___

I'd ___ find ___ my - self ___ drown -
how could so ___ much love ___ be ___

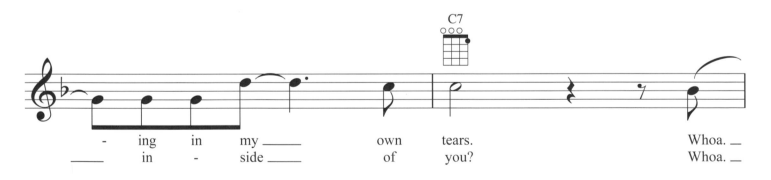

- ing in my ___ own tears. Whoa. ___
- in - side ___ of you? Whoa. ___

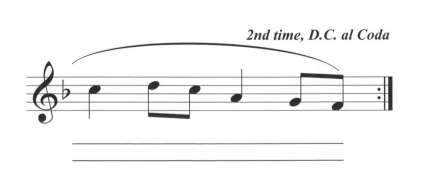

2nd time, D.C. al Coda

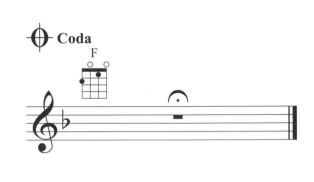

Coda